Katie
AND
Alex
The Love Story

EMILY HERBERT

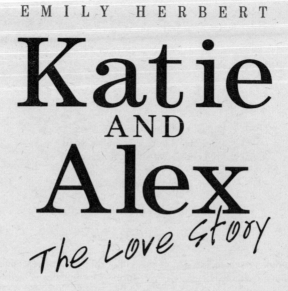

Katie
AND
Alex
The Love Story

JOHN BLAKE

Published by John Blake Publishing Ltd,
3 Bramber Court, 2 Bramber Road,
London W14 9PB, England

www.johnblakepublishing.co.uk

First published in paperback in 2010

ISBN: 978-1-84358-181-9

British Library Cataloguing-in-Publication Data:

A catalogue record for this book is available from the British Library.

Printed in Great Britain by CPI Bookmarque, Croydon, CR0 4TD

1 3 5 7 9 10 8 6 4 2

Papers used by John Blake Publishing are natural, recyclable products made
from wood grown in sustainable forests. The manufacturing processes
conform to the environmental regulations of the country of origin.

Every attempt has been made to contact the relevant copyright-holders,
but some were unobtainable. We would be grateful if the appropriate people
could contact us.

CONTENTS

CHAPTER 1

A MARRIAGE MADE IN VEGAS

The news, when it came, was so surprising, so stunning, that even in the chaotically driven, upside-down world that is the life of Katie Price, at first no one could be sure it was true. Just two months after dumping her boyfriend Alex Reid and less than six months after her divorce from Peter Andre, Katie and Alex had got married in Las Vegas.

In stark contrast to her nuptials with Peter, which featured a Cinderella theme, complete with vast glass coach and fairytale outfit, this ceremony was quick and private, and although a television crew was in evidence filming for Katie's reality TV show, this time there was no celebrity magazine. The couple had travelled to Las Vegas to celebrate Alex's triumph in *Celebrity Big Brother*, but no one had expected a celebration like this.

Katie and Alex were married. It was a stunning end to an extremely turbulent six months.

The ceremony itself took place in the Wynn Hotel at 4pm local time, on 2 February 2010, in a venue close to where they were staying: the five-star Planet Hollywood hotel on Sunset Strip. The chapel was bedecked with roses; the ceremony itself took a mere 22 minutes before the duo were pronounced man and wife. Just a couple of hours earlier, they had given a hint as to what they were planning next when they were spotted shopping for rings at a nearby jeweller; shortly after the ceremony they confirmed what had just taken place.

'Katie and Alex are delighted to announce that they got married in a private, simple ceremony at 4pm (PST) on February 2nd in Las Vegas,' they said in a statement. 'We are very much in love and look forward to the future together. We can't wait to get back and celebrate our marriage with our friends and family, who we know fully support our wishes.'

As for the lack of a magazine deal – although that certainly couldn't be ruled out for the future – 'Their decision to marry has not been made with any pre-conceived commercial plan or media deal in place, and their reason for getting married is purely down to their love for each other,' said their spokesman. So this was it: the next logical step in a love story that started out in an even greater blaze of publicity than Katie's romance with her first husband, Peter Andre. Katie and Alex were in love and now they were married. What more was there to say?

Well, actually, quite a lot. No magazine had been present, but there was a strong possibility that a further ceremony might be staged once the couple were back in the UK, under the constant glare of the cameras with which they had conducted their relationship so far. And while magazine cameras might not have been in situ, others were still there.

'Her ITV2 camera crew were with her and could well have filmed the wedding,' said an insider at the event. 'But Katie is not sure yet whether she will allow the footage to be aired. She has not signed any magazine deal for the wedding photographs, but they are likely to do an interview about it when they get back.'

The signals were certainly mixed. Just days before the wedding, Katie had appeared on Alan Carr's *Chatty Man* show and told him: 'I don't feel I have to tell the press and media everything that I do. I don't want us to be seen in the public eye now. I just want to keep it separate. I said to Alex, "OK, to prove that we're together and no one around you is using me for publicity or you to get anywhere, I don't want us to be seen in the public eye now."'

Naturally, this had to be taken with a pinch of salt. After all, Katie's camera crew was in attendance, as it always was, and it was looking increasingly likely that the couple would do some further media outing about their nuptials (or indeed, hold another ceremony) on their return to the UK. But it was certainly the case that the constant gaze of the media had done Katie's relationship with Pete no favours at all.

Indeed, he had already said in so many words that allowing the camera to film their every move had been a mistake and that with hindsight, they should have allowed themselves more privacy and this may well have played a part in Katie's calculations about what to do next. But in truth, she'd been living her life in front of the cameras for years – there was no way she could go back to absolute privacy now.

At the ceremony itself, Katie was wearing an elegant off-white dress, while in attendance were her closest friends Gary Cockerill and Phill Turner, her publicist Diana Colbert and two friends of Alex's. Once they had exchanged their vows, the couple kissed passionately and headed off to celebrate – along with shopping for a ring, they had also been spotted purchasing sex toys at the Déjà Vu 'love clinic'.

There was certainly no denying they made a very happy pair. Both gave every appearance of being over the moon: although their eight-month romance had certainly had its ups and downs, the two had clearly reached a new stage in their feelings towards one another. 'Kate was incredibly excited,' revealed another source close to the scene. 'She had the idea while Alex was in the *Celebrity Big Brother* house and decided to just run with it. She loves Alex, and he is great with her three kids, so she thought she'd go for it.

'They may have secured a lucrative deal for the rights to their wedding, but their love is genuine. Alex worships the ground she walks on and Kate fancies the pants off him. They wanted to have the ceremony as soon as they got to Vegas, but the bridal stores weren't open so she couldn't get a dress. She had her fashion team trawling all over town for a gown. In the end she just had to make do. It was nothing like the last time, when she'd spent months designing her perfect dress. Her last wedding – with all her celeb pals and a huge fuss – ended in disaster. Kate wanted a no-nonsense do this time, with just her nearest and dearest. She's a savvy businesswoman and decided she may as well get paid to get married.'

In truth, Katie never really 'made do' and a wardrobe as extensive as hers was bound to turn up something suitable. But it was a big day and a big occasion, and she understandably wanted to look her best.

Alex himself was over the moon. Coming right after his *Big Brother* win, this was both a chance to cement his relationship with the woman he loved and the culmination of a remarkable phase in his life.

'It's been a fantastic start to the New Year and it's going to be even more fantastic now this is happening,' he commented. 'I actually asked Katie to marry me after my fight in September, so it's something we've been discussing for some time. I hope the public learns something from this. Four weeks ago I was the bad guy getting booed, now they're cheering me.'

Katie certainly seemed to be taking it all very seriously, even insisting she'd be changing her surname. 'I'll change my passport, cheque book, everything,' she said. 'I want to be traditional, the way a marriage is meant to be.'

But was that really practical? Katie already existed under several different names – Jordan and Katie Price – and would introducing a third into the mix not dilute the brand? But these days, anything seemed possible in the world of Katie Price.

It certainly was quite a turnaround. Ever since her split from her first husband, Katie had been very aware that public opinion had not been on her side and when the relationship with Alex first began, there was real hostility towards him, but that was changing and the fact that Pete felt able to give the duo his blessing didn't hurt either.

'As long as there's a good influence for the kids, I'm happy,' he said on the Chris Moyles show on Radio 1. 'I don't have any negative feelings inside me. As long as they're happy, great.'

Nonetheless, the couple continued the slightly unconventional approach to their nuptials the next day. They visited a series of strip clubs, including Sapphire Gentleman's Club, with Katie sporting black latex trousers and a fur gilet. There were reports that it got a little fruity, with Katie complaining that Alex had become too engrossed in the antics of one particular lapdancer called Lexi: 'Maybe we got married too soon!' she was heard to say, before Alex made it up to her by buying her very own lap dance, followed by more passionate embracing.

'Kate and Alex are a lively duo,' said a witness to the scene. 'They'd only been married about seven hours when they had their first row, and it wasn't pretty. Alex was drooling over a lapdancer and Kate gave him a stern telling-off.

'She declared, "Maybe we've married too soon" before turning on her high heels. Alex apologised profusely and within minutes the pair were once again lovers, not fighters.'

After that it was a return to their £6,300-a-night penthouse suite, where they ordered room service from Koi, the hotel's Japanese restaurant: the feast comprised oysters, rock shrimp, crispy rice with tuna and a chocolate cake with berries, washed down with two bottles of Dom Perignon at an eyewatering £315 a bottle. A 'Do Not Disturb' sign went up on the bedroom door: 'It's time to get cracking on a honeymoon baby!' said Katie happily. 'Bring it on!'

The next day, they went dune buggying in the Nevada desert. Katie initially looked nervous, but soon afterwards, in a move which many felt reflected what might well be the true state of the relationship, she took charge. Nonetheless, the two were clearly besotted with one another: 'Kate and Alex are so happy,' said a source close to the couple. 'They have been laughing and joking almost non-stop since exchanging vows, and really are in love. Their strength is they have a real giggle, and that's why they decided to get tipsy in a strip club. Why shouldn't they? They didn't want a pompous wedding and didn't make their first night a staid one, either. They returned to their suite for some privacy and a romantic candlelit dinner. Alex has made no secret of the fact he wants a child too, so they are hoping to conceive as quickly as possible. Kate's said "never underestimate the Pricey – I conceive easily!" Alex thinks all his Christmases have come at once.'

Even so, there were already reports of some sniping at one another afoot. 'Katie has been very difficult to manage,' revealed a source close to the couple. 'She has been walking around with a face like thunder a lot of the time. She and Alex are also bickering over where to go when they leave Vegas at the end of the week. Poor Alex is getting it in the neck already.'

The issue of where they would go next was a real one. Shortly after the wedding, Alex was due in India to film his new TV show for cable channel Bravo, and this couple, of all couples, knew that work always came first. He was also busy training: he was due to fight Tom 'Kong' Watson, the UK's current Middleweight Ultimate Challenge World Champion, and as such was travelling to six different countries to learn six different fighting styles. In India, this was to be Kushti, which was Indian wrestling, and Marma Adi.

Katie was not supposed to tag along: she would, after all, be a distraction and no one, especially Bravo, wanted that. 'Alex has to train hard and have no distractions, there is no glitz at his Indian training camp,' said a source. 'He has to be focused to win, and Jordan has been told she cannot come with him to India, so she is going to Los Angeles for work. The production team are primed for Jordan to have a bit of a hissy fit, though, and fly out there anyway. It's not much of a honeymoon, that's for sure.'

But it was the way the two of them operated for, just as she had with Pete, Katie was beginning to discover that she and Alex were worth far more together than apart. Certainly, they loved one another, but they were also acutely aware that to stay in the public eye, they needed to be constantly moving on and engaging in new projects. If this meant that Alex had to go to India, while Katie jetted off to LA, so be it. It kept them in the public eye, and both were keen to continue with that just for now.

Not everything was going entirely smoothly, however. Back in the UK, Pete's initial *laissez-faire* attitude was shaken when he appeared on television in a live interview with Kay Burley, who pushed him very hard about the role Alex would play in his children's lives. He remained calm about Alex himself: 'I don't know the man, I've never met him,' he said. 'I couldn't care less, I'm sorry, I'm not being bitter.' In fact, the children, Junior and Princess, were not yet aware that their mother had remarried: 'I guess it's something that I'm going to have to explain to them,' he said.

But the tone of the interview then changed quite sharply. Kay began to ask him about the nature of his relationship with Harvey, who was now seven, Katie's son with the footballer, Dwight Yorke: Harvey had always regarded Pete as being his father, something that had begun to annoy Dwight. Kay played an interview with Dwight, in which he described Pete's request to adopt Harvey as 'disrespectful' and Pete started to become visibly distressed. 'I asked to adopt him because I love him, not to be disrespectful,' he said. 'That angers me a little bit.'

It was a fair point: Pete had been Harvey's *de facto* father for years, and there was nothing in his relationship with the child that equated to Alex's relationship with his, Pete's, children. Nonetheless, Kay asked how Pete would feel if Alex wanted to adopt Junior and Princess, the children Pete had fathered with Katie.

'No one is going to take my kids away from me,' he said, clearly upset. 'And I will fight to the death for that. Nobody is going to take those kids away from me. It's not going to happen.' By now visibly distressed, he wanted to end the interview: 'I'd rather just stop this, if that's alright.'

But the interview did not go unnoticed by Pete fans, who were livid at all of this. In the wake of the break-up, he had behaved with a huge amount of dignity and his supporters were not happy at what they saw as such an insensitive line in questioning. Almost immediately, a Facebook campaign was launched, calling for Kay to be sacked, which attracted nearly 3,000 signatures. Meanwhile, Kay herself professed to be shamefaced at the way it had gone.

'What a day,' she wrote later on her blog. 'Peter Andre broke down on my show and when I went to check during an ad break that he was okay, he sobbed on my shoulder in the Green Room. He'd discovered not 12 hours earlier that the mother of two of his children had married without even bothering to tell him and was devastated at the very thought that she might want to take the youngsters away from him. I was mortified at having upset such an obviously doting family man and was keen to offer sincere apologies, but he was his usual charming self.'

Back in Las Vegas, Katie was showing off her new wedding ring for the first time – a £60,000 thickset platinum band adorned with diamonds, as opposed to the £350,000 ring she'd received from Pete. It was from the Las Vegas-based TeNo jeweller: 'In keeping with their quick, unflashy wedding, Kate didn't want a showy diamond ring,' said a source. 'She wanted something plain, something she can wear all the time, even when she is horseriding. It's not flashy at all, but both she and Alex love it. Katie could not be happier.'

On the flight back to the UK, the party continued. 'Let's just say Alex and Katie enjoyed quite a steamy session on the flight back from Las Vegas,' a friend of the pair revealed. 'The plane had hardly taken off before Katie had snuggled up to Alex on his first-class bed – and they were literally at it for 12 hours. Katie's never been shy in the sack, even if she's a mile high with other passengers just yards away. It seemed they had a bit of making up to do after a couple of post-wedding rows in Vegas.' Could a newly married couple be any happier than this?

But not everyone was convinced. Some onlookers believed it to be all a well-thought up publicity stunt – and if it was, given the media attention they were attracting, it was certainly working – not least because shortly after their return to the UK, Alex was off again to Mumbai. 'The fact that Alex and Katie are not even spending their first married night back in the UK together will raise a lot of eyebrows,' a source commented. 'The whole thing reeks of being one massive publicity stunt. What Jordan is doing with Alex seems almost a carbon copy of what she did with Peter Andre five years ago.'

That wasn't quite fair. Katie and Pete had met in the *I'm A Celebrity...* jungle and theirs had been a rather lengthier courtship: the two did not get together immediately after emerging from the trees, playing something of a cat-and-mouse game until they were sure the other was really interested, and the marriage didn't take place until 18 months after they'd met. But what both relationships undoubtedly had in common was the ability to attract attention. There was quite as much fascination with Katie and Alex as there had ever been with Katie and Pete.

It was not quite clear if Alex's advisors could see that, however. He had been whisked off to Mumbai at the earliest possible opportunity, with dark hints that Katie might be holding him back – although if truth be told, without her there would have been no public interest in him whatsoever. 'Alex's people believe he has not had the chance to fully capitalise on his *Celebrity Big*

Brother win,' said a source. 'In their opinion Jordan is manipulative and has hijacked all their hard work. As soon as Alex won *CBB* she whisked him off to Las Vegas to get married without a moment's notice. There was no chance for him to speak to his agents about the projects and plans they had laid on for him, not to mention the trip to India. She just seems to be able to wind Alex round her little finger.'

She was certainly planning for the future and it looked increasingly likely another ceremony would be the order of the day. After all, her children (along with various magazines) had not been present at the ceremony and Katie was now talking about including them, too. 'Jordan wants to get married again so her family, close friends and, most importantly, her kids can see her making a commitment to Alex,' said a friend. 'She thinks it's important the kids are there to help them understand that Alex is her new husband.'

The children were, in fact, proving to be an increasing bone of contention. Pete's early acceptance of the situation didn't appear to be lasting: he was now letting it be known that he didn't think Alex should be allowed to profit from his children, and if truth be told, already there was a precedent. In the extremely bitter aftermath of the split, Katie and Pete had both been filming their own reality television shows, but while Junior and Princess, Pete's two biological children, were free to appear on his series, Harvey could not. This was because he was not Pete's biological child, and Pete needed Katie to give her permission to allow Harvey to appear on the screen, which she was not prepared to do.

Now it appeared that the situation might be reversed. Pete was extremely unhappy at the idea that Junior and Princess might appear on an Alex reality television show and he was determined to do his utmost to make sure they did not. 'Pete has been on the phone to his lawyers, trying to sort this out,' revealed a friend. 'He is furious at any suggestion Alex might play more of a role in the children's lives. His worst nightmare would be turning on the TV and having to watch Alex playing with his kids.' Nor was Pete quite as sanguine about the wedding as he had previously appeared: he was letting it be known that he considered it to have been 'tasteless'. Trouble was clearly afoot.

Rather surprisingly, given the tensions between them, Katie actually stood up for Pete, especially where the Kay Burley interview was concerned. She felt, understandably, that Pete had played a considerably more significant role in Harvey's life than his biological father, Dwight Yorke, and whatever she herself might have felt towards her former husband, she conceded that he was an excellent father. Nor, she countered, did she and Alex have any intention of depriving Pete of his children.

'It's disgusting how Pete was treated,' she said. 'Pete's an amazing dad to Harvey. He's his dad, and always will be. It upset me that they compared the two because Dwight has never played the role of dad in Harvey's life. Alex has no intention of adopting the kids. We're dying to have our own and I hope that by the end of this show [her reality show, *What Katie Did Next*] I can announce I'm pregnant, so watch out for the bump. And after our own, we want to adopt. It's more important to have my family life and husband than fame. I realise it's not about being paid for interviews. Hopefully, one day he'll [Pete] come round. He will have kids with his girlfriend and we'll all be able to play happy families like my mum and dad did when they split up. But at the moment Pete and I are not speaking. We haven't, really, since the jungle.' But at least she was being generous towards him, which was a start.

Matters were soon made worse, however: this time from very different quarters, extremely concerned as to what Katie would do now. For obvious reasons, Katie's family had been on her side, but right from the start of the split from Pete, they were anxious that her behaviour might cause serious problems. In the immediate aftermath of the split, she had run wild, larging it in Ibiza and very nearly destroying her reputation in the process, and now they were very worried about her latest marriage to a highly controversial figure – cross-dressing cage fighters were not obvious husband material – and what the implications might be.

Katie's mother Amy was particularly concerned. One friend reported her as telling her daughter: 'This is completely pathetic – you are no longer a young woman with no children to think about, you have responsibilities. This is a silly, silly thing to do!'

Other reports had it that she was totally exasperated with the way things were turning out. 'Amy is at her wits' end with Katie,' revealed a friend. 'She has tried to tell her time and again that she needs to grow up and put her children first. Although Alex and Katie have been together for seven months, she feels there was no thought of the repercussions from the wedding. What irritates Amy most is that Katie didn't put much thought into it, which proves she doesn't have respect for the vows she has taken. Amy feels that if Katie ought to have learned anything from her split from Pete it is that getting married is a big deal.' One newspaper asked her what it felt like to have a new son-in-law: 'I don't know,' she replied. 'You tell me.'

Nor was Katie's brother Danny happy about the situation. Danny was a couple of years older than his sister and had managed her finances throughout her career, so he had always been close to her, with her best interests at heart. He was also pretty upset by it all. 'This is just for money,' he is reputed to have told her. 'I've been there for you through the hard times and this is how you repay it.'

Even Katie's younger half-sister Sophie was upset, although in this case it was because she hadn't played a bigger role on the day. Another report had it that Sophie burst into tears when Katie rang with the news: 'But you said I could be your bridesmaid,' she wept. Katie reassured her that there would soon be another ceremony and that Sophie was to play a big role in it.

It was hardly an auspicious start to married life, and it wasn't just Katie's family who were concerned: Alex's parents Carol and Bob were, too. Quite apart from anything else, it had happened so very, very quickly, and they weren't sure what to make of it all.

'Are you sure you're not being taken for a ride?' they are said to have asked him. 'Don't you think you should have waited a bit longer? You're no longer a teenager.' That he wasn't, but for better or worse, the deed had been done.

Then it was back to Pete. Katie had caused huge controversy by allowing Princess, who was still only two, to appear in full make-up. The pictures, which were posted on Sophie's Facebook page, caused uproar and Pete was at the forefront of it all.

'Well, to be honest, or to be lying? If I'm going to be honest, I'm absolutely disgusted,' he told GMTV. 'And to me, that is the worst thing to be worried about. It's a two-year-old girl and she's – for the whole world to see – dressed like that. And to me, I think that's disgusting. It's a two-year-old girl with false eyelashes on, full of make-up, for the whole world to see. To be honest with you, I'm disgusted – that's it. I don't really think there's really anymore to say.'

He did not, however, wish to contact his ex about it: 'If I pick up a phone, what will be said will not remain private,' he continued. 'So therefore I won't. But you know, usually I come on, I don't – you know – I just talk about other things, and I'm like, "Yeah, I'm not bothered and all this," but that did bother me.'

Katie, needless to say, was not going to take it lying down. 'If I am such a bad mum then I would have been reported to Social Services,' she snapped. 'We have a nurse who works for Great Ormond Street and works for us three times a week. She is the nurse if children come in and are abused, then she reports them to Social Services, so I am sure she would report me if I was a bad mum. I am a good mum, I know I am.'

Despite this, she did, however, continue to attempt to build bridges with Pete. Valentine's Day came round, and Katie agreed that he should spend it with the children.

'I won't be lonely at all – I'm spending the day with my own Princess,' he declared. Indeed, he planned on giving them lesson in how to make cupcakes: 'He's been out and bought ingredients,' said his spokeswoman. 'Pete's so delighted he got the kids.'

The public maintained a palpable warmth towards him: whatever everyone thought about Katie and Alex – and it wasn't at all clear what the general mood would turn out to be – Pete was as popular as ever. He was a good man, he loved his children and he was determined to do right by them, that much was clear even if nothing else in this convoluted saga could be said to be so.

Katie, meanwhile, was spending Valentine's Day with her new husband and reported the event on Twitter: '*WOW three huge boxes turned up...my husband really has spoilt me for valentines day he is just PERFECT...i love you husband amazing.*' Someone was happy, at least.

Throughout all this, Alex had been remarkably quiet, but now he was determined to have his say. He and Katie were married, after all, and while everyone else had been making their feelings clear, he had been rather left in the background. Now it was time his turn to make a stand. 'Katie said in various interviews last week that we're already trying for a baby,' he said. 'And I can confirm that we did lots of practising in Vegas! I really can't wait to become a dad – and I'll be thrilled whether we have a boy or a girl, whenever it happens.'

As for any family tensions – 'My mum and family are 100 per cent behind us and are delighted we got married,' he continued. 'They all know how incredible

Katie is, and we will celebrate with all of our family and friends in the UK soon. I am still feeling so happy. It has finally all sunk in now, and being married to Mrs Reid is the most amazing thing in the world. The only bad bit has been having to remove my wedding ring when I'm fighting! I don't like that at all.'

At least he and Katie were happy, but it had all seemed so very different between the pair just three short months ago.

CHAPTER 2

NOT EVERYONE'S CUP OF TEA

Katie and Alex were married. Any doubters who thought their relationship was just another publicity stunt had been shown that it was far more than that. In getting married, not only had they shown their commitment towards one another but they had also very publicly overcome the various travails that beset them as a couple right from the start.

Indeed, they had had an extremely rocky start to their relationship, which many believed had begun indecently soon after Katie's split from Pete, nor had they appeared certain where the two of them wanted to go next. Almost certainly, Katie was still on the rebound when she and Alex got together, for her distress at Pete's departure was palpable. Alex, meanwhile, not only found himself suddenly in a world unlike anything he had ever experienced before, but he had also been subjected to a series of vitriolic attacks from a couple of his former girlfriends. It was a lot to take on board.

Indeed, just three months earlier, things were very different. Towards the beginning of November 2009, Katie and Alex had become an established couple, but the relationship was frequently turbulent. Revelations that Katie's new partner was a cage fighter who had recently enjoyed a starring role in a violent film of a sexual nature – 2010's *Killer Babe* – had ruffled some feathers, and the fact that he was a cross dresser hadn't gone down well in some quarters, either. On top of that, public opinion was still polarised between Katie and Pete.

Katie had had a tumultuous time of it since the split the previous May: although she clearly felt that public opinion should be on her side, given that it was Pete who initiated the split and not her, in actual fact, the opposite had been the case.

Katie had emerged from the marriage and run wild, partying in Ibiza and at times appearing semi-naked; even when Alex appeared on the scene, she had been pictured frolicking with him in front of her children, much to the public's disgust. Pete, on the other hand, had played a blinder: he refused to criticise her in public, he did not appear with a string of new women on his arm, he put in a serious amount of time and effort in looking after the children and gave every appearance of being the devoted father. There was never any suggestion that Katie was anything but a loving mother, but she had gone about the recovery process in a completely different way.

Given this background, it was perhaps not too surprising that, as Katie and Alex settled not entirely harmoniously into coupledom, threats were made against the pair. Not only this, but they were also made towards Katie's horses. Along with her children, this was her weak point: she was famously devoted to her animals – if anyone wanted to hurt her, this was an obvious target. Indeed, the threats were malicious and unfortunately, very real. 'Katie was very upset when she found out about the threats,' revealed a friend. 'She realises she and Alex are not everybody's cup of tea, but really can't believe someone could be so cruel. She is petrified for Alex and absolutely terrified someone is going to hurt her horses – they mean the world to her.'

One of the reasons why the threats came to light in the first place was that Alex was logged on to a Mixed Martial Arts website discussion board containing some very odd and threatening posts. Rather unwisely perhaps, he engaged the man in virtual chat, which simply allowed matters to escalate, so much so that the situation threatened to get totally out of hand. 'Alex decided to reply and say it was out of order as the man didn't know him,' the friend continued. 'But this led the guy to start posting more threats, including one which said he would even kill Katie's horses.'

It was at this point that the couple decided to alert the authorities. 'The threats have been really nasty,' the friend continued. 'But it's the threat to kill her horses that made the most impact – it's like something out of *The Godfather*. Police have been called and a complaint has been made. Katie is just doing her best to move forward, but it can't help but be a worry.'

Hampshire Police did, indeed, get involved. 'Yesterday evening we attended an address in Aldershot after receiving information relating to inappropriate and threatening comments that were made on a website,' said a spokesman. 'They have caused some concern. We are continuing to make some inquiries around these reports.'

After the initial worry, however, matters began to die down. Katie was no stranger to controversy and clearly felt that the best way forward was to ignore what was going on, not least because publicising the couple's woes might simply exacerbate the situation. If whoever was making the threats was getting a kick out of worrying Katie and Alex, then going public would just encourage him. 'A storm in a teacup,' declared Katie dismissively, although she did add: 'Please leave my horses alone – like my children, they are my life.' In the event that was the end of the matter, but Katie and Alex were being forced to deal with confrontation on a regular basis now. On another occasion, after attending a fight, an onlooker lashed out at Alex. It may have gone with the territory, but it was wearisome, all the same.

Despite, or perhaps because of all these problems rumbling away in the background, the relationship continued to be fractious. The threats might have drawn the pair closer together: instead, at that stage at least, they merely pushed them apart. There were reports of rows and reconciliations, of jealousies, squabbles and making up. The very air around them seemed to be at a heightened emotional pitch – even if she had wanted a quiet life (and Katie had never shown much inclination for that), it was the last thing she was getting. Indeed, her ability to turn everyday life into a commotion was now operating as never before.

But what would happen next? How would their relationship develop in the midst of all this? Neither really appeared to know what they wanted at this stage when every incident seemed to turn into a drama. Always eager to dive into any new project, whether work or love, Katie had been floating the idea that they should cement their relationship with tattoos, an idea about which she now appeared increasingly doubtful. Was Alex really her next great love or just a fling? At this stage it was not at all clear. And then there was the fact that Katie and Pete had had tattoos of one another's name as well (Katie had famously had hers crossed out with a black ink tattoo). Was it really a good idea for Alex to be seen to be stepping so very closely into his predecessor's shoes? Besides, the two men could hardly have been more different, so was it wise to give the critics such direct ammunition when it had a real chance of blowing up in Alex's face?

The tattoo question surfaced around the time that Katie headed off to the Bloodlust Halloween Ball at Hampton Court House in Surrey in early November and caused a number of greater than usual rows. First, one of them blew hot and then cold about the idea, then the other blew cold followed by hot. And while this was hardly the most serious of topics to disagree on, it was just another indication that the relationship was not running smoothly at that point.

'It must be something in the air around Halloween,' observed a source close to the pair. 'Katie and Alex have been bickering about this for a while. A few months back, Katie told Alex she wanted to get the tattoos – just like she did with Peter Andre. The problem was, Alex was not keen at first. It was early days and he was not sure. As you can imagine, this put Jordan's nose right out of joint. She accused Alex of not being committed to her. Then he turned round and said, "OK, I'll have the tattoo done." But Katie is not interested now.'

Of course, the relationship was still a very new one, with neither yet sure about where it was going to go, but this had all the hallmarks of Katie: on the one hand desperate for reassurance that it was all very serious, yet disinterested as soon as she'd got what she wanted. At that point, it was impossible for either of them to know where they stood.

But the tattoo dilemma was brushed firmly aside almost immediately afterwards, when Harvey was rushed into hospital with a high fever, forcing Katie and Pete to set aside their differences and race to his side. Harvey was taken to A&E at the East Surrey Hospital in Redhill, where doctors said he must stay until they were certain about what was causing the problem. This was just the latest in a long line of problems – Harvey suffers from septo-optic dysplasia, meaning he is blind, and he is also on the autistic spectrum and finds walking difficult – and it served as a reminder that whatever heightened emotional issues Harvey's parents might be dealing with, his own issues were not going to go away. Dwight Yorke, Harvey's biological father, had played little part in his son's life, and now it was Pete, as ever, who was called on to step into the breach. Pete all but regarded Harvey as his own, hence his deep distress in reference to his relationship with the children – no matter how many squabbles he might have with Katie, that would never change.

And Harvey was extremely ill. He needed his parents, who were dreadfully concerned about what was happening to their child. 'Harvey had a massive temperature and couldn't keep any food down either,' revealed a friend. 'More worryingly, his breathing was also a huge concern and there was no option but to urgently seek medical advice. The doctors weren't taking any chances. If he doesn't get any better, he might be there for a while. It could well be complications arising from potential swine flu, but they don't know yet. He's a very poorly young man.'

With Harvey's general state of health not so good as it could have been, let alone when he had episodes like this, this was cause for real concern. Indeed, Katie cancelled everything: 'I have to be there for Harvey,' she said. 'He's my little angel and he needs his mummy.'

But this was far from being his first health scare and it prompted a thorough investigation into what had gone wrong. Harvey would never be completely free of these issues and to their immense credit, Katie and Pete did everything in their power to make sure the little boy was all right: 'When it comes to Harvey's health, even little coughs and colds are treated very seriously,' said a friend. 'That is why Kate is deeply worried.'

Pete, of course, was in situ. At that point, he and Katie could agree on very little, but the health of their child was something else and they were totally united in their concern. 'Doctors decided to keep him in overnight for observation as a precautionary measure,' Katie's spokesman revealed. 'Katie was in touch with Peter from the moment it was decided to take Harvey in.' In the event, Harvey made a full recovery, but it was a salutary reminder that there were more important issues than tattoos at stake.

Meanwhile, Katie's relationship with Alex was unsettled. Both remained under intense media scrutiny, yet neither was sure of the future. In the heightened dramatic atmosphere surrounding their every move, everything felt as if it were at extremes: there was no grey area, only black and white. There didn't even seem to be any room to take the relationship slowly: it was all or it was nothing. And so it was hardly surprising that at this stage it looked as though the couple might split.

It was at this point that Alex began to plan the tour that would, in fact, begin immediately after the wedding, but at that stage not only were there no wedding bells in evidence, but some people believe he saw it as a much-needed break. After all, his life had changed completely in the months since he'd met Katie. Although he had been on the peripheries of show business for some time, with roles in *Soldier, Soldier* and *Hollyoaks* during the late 1990s, as well as acting as a stand-in for Tom Hanks in *Saving Private Ryan*, now he was in a whole new world.

From being almost a complete unknown, he now received as much press coverage as his new girlfriend: his face and name were becoming familiar to every newspaper and magazine reader in the land. And while this had its advantages, it was not totally without setbacks: with fame, comes pressure. Threats had been made against him and there was also constant carping from the media, to say nothing of the inevitable comparisons with the saintly Peter Andre. Alex would not have been human if he hadn't sometimes felt the weight of all that pressure and briefly, it seemed as if he felt he needed an escape. And then there was his career. Alex Reid was no longer primarily known as being a cage fighter: his main role in life appeared to be as Katie Price's boyfriend and it took a strong man to be able to deal with that.

And so the only solution, according to some people, was to take off. 'He's had enough,' said a friend. 'He's decided to fuck off round the world. He just can't stand it any more. "Escape" is the right word. Alex enjoyed himself to start with, but now the relationship has become a living nightmare. He is really feeling the stress of it all. He hopes that, by going away, he can put Katie and the strain of being with her out of his mind and repair himself mentally. Alex's cage fighting has taken a knock since he's been with Katie because he doesn't have the right environment to prepare in. He hopes he can get his preparation back, so he can become a better fighter. He is going to stick it out here over Christmas and the New Year, but after that, he's off. He needs the time alone.'

Indeed, the constant attention was getting him down. It requires a particular kind of nerve to be able to live in the limelight and while Katie could manage it, in her case, she'd learned how to handle the pressure over the years. She had not, after all, been catapulted to centre stage. She'd had a couple of years of falling out of nightclubs before people really began to twig who she was. Alex had had none of that: he'd been pitched in at the deep end, and was having to learn how to cope – and fast.

Then there was his career. While all the exposure was hardly going to hurt him, Alex had not actually been doing a great deal of cage fighting recently and he was concerned his own standards were beginning to drop. For all that he enjoyed being with his new girlfriend, he refused to make it his job to be Katie Price's boyfriend and he was beginning to worry that his fans would forget him. Time away seemed the ideal solution.

'Basically, Alex just wants to get away from the circus that is Jordan,' the friend continued. 'At first he loved all the cameras and attention, but now he has told his mates he has had enough. He says the trip is to cleanse his mind and build up his strength so he can keep his cage fighting career going. Without that he knows he has no future for himself once he splits from Jordan. When he's with her he stays out late and hardly trains. He has told pals his life is a mess and he really needs to get into a better place.'

But what were Katie's thoughts on all this? She was used to being in control in a relationship and having had Pete recently walk out on her, she was hardly going to be happy if the same thing happened again with Alex. And this relationship was, if anything, even more high profile than the one with Pete. How did she feel about Alex's idea to suddenly take off on a tour around the world? Not positive, that was for sure. She was still very raw, very vulnerable, and clearly she wanted a man who could give her moral support.

'Jordan wasn't happy, especially when he asked her to help pay for the trip, and they exchanged angry words,' said the friend. 'To be honest, I'd be surprised if they are even still together when Valentine's Day comes around.'

That prediction was to prove a little wide of the mark but even so, it was an indication that both were feeling the strain. Of course Katie had been exposed to that kind of pressure for years, but even she seemed wearied by events and she was also wondering whether her new relationship was turning out as what she had hoped. 'Secretly, she'd be happy to see the back of him for a while,' said a friend. 'All they seem to do at the moment is needle each other.'

Neither, however, would make an official statement: 'He could have plans to travel next year, but whether it's on his own or with Katie, we can't comment,' said a spokesperson for the couple and that was all anyone was prepared to say for now. But in actual fact, of course, events were moving so fast that the pair were now caught up in a swirl of activity over which even they seemed to have little control any more. It was always a moot point in the world of Katie Price as to whether she was setting the agenda or whether it was setting her: either way, even by her own high standards, the drama that was her life was as eventful as never before. In that way, at least, she had found a worthy successor to Pete – whether he wanted to do so or not, Alex was quite as capable of stirring up drama as his new paramour and playing a leading role in the soap opera that had become their lives.

But it wasn't an easy position to be in, and the constant comparisons with Pete didn't help, either. The very different way in which Katie's ex-husband was coping with the split was emphasised more and more: far from moving on to another relationship, as Katie had done, Pete wasn't ready for so much as a fling. And like it or not, the public respected that: Pete was a family man who had found it enormously difficult to make the split from Katie and he was unhappy about starting a new relationship while everything else was still very much up in the air. He managed, on the whole, to keep his own counsel about Alex, but he was resolute that he himself was not yet ready to move on from Katie.

But again, the difference in the behaviour of everyone concerned caused even more tensions: neither Katie nor Alex could be blamed for feeling the strain. Pete remained celibate, and was happy to talk about it, too. 'I haven't slept with any woman since Kate,' he said. 'I'm not ready and it's not right. I do want a relationship at some stage, but you can't just fling yourself into that sort of situation – that's madness. I will always love her as the mother of my children, but that is it. I'm not in love with her.'

It was over, for sure, but by virtue of the link created by their children, Katie and Pete were, in some ways, bound together forever. Even marriage to Alex wouldn't change that.

But Katie had proved time and again, when her back was up against the wall, she would come out fighting. The relationship with Alex endured – indeed, despite the rows and bickering, going through all this together would ultimately make it stronger. Meanwhile, Katie began to think about what she would do next in terms of her own career.

And she began to hatch a plan. It was when she entered the celebrity jungle in 2004 that her image had been turned around beyond her wildest dreams: back then, she had entered the jungle as Jordan, left as Katie Price, found herself a husband and become a national treasure into the bargain. The producers of *I'm A Celebrity... Get Me Out Of Here!* were currently planning their next series and putting together a list of people who would shock and excite the nation. They wanted contestants who would bring them maximum publicity. Katie, meanwhile, was beginning to think that if the real Katie was exposed to viewers on prime-time television, they would see what she was really like and stop judging her so harshly. Why not stage a return to the jungle that so comprehensively changed her life?

And there was another reason for returning to the jungle as well – namely, keeping the relationship with Alex on track. Whatever the thinking behind his future tour, Katie did not want any man to get the upper hand on her publicly, and so going off into the jungle was both a way of ensuring she remained in the spotlight and keeping Alex in line. She had, after all, met her previous husband in the jungle and who was to say she wouldn't do so again? And it has often been forgotten that when she went into the jungle on the previous occasion to meet Peter Andre, she wasn't a free agent then, either – she was actually dating Scott Sullivan, who was unceremoniously dumped as matters with Pete began to develop. Could history repeat itself? Might exactly the same thing happen again?

Katie was certainly intent on keeping her options open. She made no bones about it either, as she prepared to jet off. 'Virtually Jordan's last words to Alex were, "I hope there's some eye candy in there,"' said a friend. 'It was her way of winding him up and she certainly achieved her aim.'

Worse still, it had leaked out that one of the fellow contestants in the jungle would be Stuart Manning, who Alex knew because they had both had roles on *Hollyoaks*. To put it mildly, he was not best pleased the two were going into the jungle together, not least because it seems that his own sex life with Katie was not what it sometimes seemed. But off Katie went, leaving Alex to fret.

'He's been really paranoid since,' revealed a friend. 'He really thinks she will stray. He doesn't want to look like a fool: he regards Stuart as a rival – he is well-built, good looking and into older women. It would crush Alex if he lost Kate to anybody, but especially Stuart. Katie's only given Alex weak assurances that she will behave herself. It hasn't helped that she asked him to move back in with his mum while she is away and not to see her kids. Katie is always talking about how much she loves sex with Alex, but the poor boy isn't getting any at all. She wouldn't even have sex with him before she went off to Australia. She spent her last night on home soil with her beautician mate Julie Williams and hairdresser Gary Cockerill. Alex is a very jealous man right now.'

Of course, that was absolutely in keeping with what Katie wanted. All talk of forthcoming cage-fighting tours was now out the window, with the spotlight firmly back on Katie, just where she liked it to be. And so, with Alex firmly put in his place, Katie once more headed off into the jungle.

CHAPTER 3

BACK TO THE JUNGLE

It was the talk of television folk everywhere. Katie Price, who had been effortlessly dominating the news schedule since her split from Peter Andre just six months earlier, was on her way back to the jungle that had changed her life just five and a half short years ago. Although TV bosses were still being coy about it, it was clear that her return would provide enormous reams of publicity, both for Katie and the show itself, something that suited everyone, with the possible exception of Pete. In fact, Pete was said to be livid, for any number of reasons, of which more below.

Katie continued to prove herself to be quite the businesswoman: she negotiated a fee rumoured to be in the region of £350,000, considerably more than anyone else involved. And it was an interesting mix. Other contestants included interior decorators Colin McAllister and Justin Ryan, Kim *'How Clean Is Your House?'* Woodburn, former glamour model Samantha Fox, *Strictly* star Camilla Dallerup, former Scots footballer Colin Hendry and ex-Mis-teeq singer Sabrina Washington. As with Kerry Katona in 2004, there was the much-anticipated 'battle of the breasts', this time courtesy of the ex-Page Three girl Sam Fox, although in truth, it would never amount to much.

In the background, however, Pete was furious, for any number of reasons. For a start, he'd been asked to do the show himself and had turned it down, and this despite the fact that he had a new single, 'Unconditional', and it would have been excellent publicity. Then there was the matter of his role as a roving reporter on ITV's *This Morning*, in which he might be expected to report on the jungle – how could he possibly do that if it involved his ex-wife? Also, the fact that Katie was going to be away from her children for so long, especially at a time of upheaval, when they could be said to be needing her most. For a family man like Pete, it was just all too much.

'Pete is absolutely furious,' said a friend. 'Obviously, he hopes he'll get more access to the kids over the New Year – for him, this is a silver lining. But he feels like he's been left in the dark about childcare. Pete turned the programme down – he thought going back on smacked slightly of desperation and he is bemused by Katie's decision to go back – it's not as if she needs the money or the profile. Also, he's concerned about the timing of the show. Harvey has been extremely poorly and Katie will be away for a month. Who's going to look after him?'

Of course, matters between the two were now at such a low that whatever Katie decided to do would probably have incurred her ex-husband's wrath, and childcare was not really a problem. Apart from Pete himself, Katie's mother Amy often helped out, plus there was no shortage of nannies and other aides. As for Katie, she saw this as an opportunity for onscreen redemption, a chance to remind the world that she was not a brazen slapper but a concerned mum who had just gone through a very tricky divorce.

'Katie decided to go for it,' said a friend. 'She loved it first time and figured it would give the public another chance to see the "real her" – and an opportunity to claw back some good PR. She'll give everything a go if it helps her look good in front of the public. Kangaroo testicles, crocodile penis – she'll give it a whirl.'

And in truth, this was yet another round of the battle between Katie and Pete that had been going on for months now. For all that it had been Pete who walked out and Katie who had got together with another partner, neither gave the impression that they had moved on – indeed, to hear them, it seemed as if they were quite as obsessed with one another as they ever had been, except now it was in an increasingly negative way. As Katie prepared to go back into the jungle, Pete chose this moment to give a long interview, detailing the pain he'd felt since the split.

'When we split up, I couldn't even look at myself in the mirror and I locked myself in my manager's house for five weeks,' he revealed. 'All my confidence vanished and I felt so anxious and stressed out that my appetite disappeared and I could barely eat. I dropped nearly three stone in three months – I went from 13st 8lb to 10st 12lb.'

The weight loss, however, had had the effect of making him feel happier about himself. In his heyday the first time round, as a pop star in the 1990s, Pete had been a very lithe creature, and now his appearance was making him once again feel as happy as he had done in the past. It wasn't just Katie who was looking for a new start: he was, too, and his changed appearance was making him feel much better about himself.

'Once I lost the weight, though, I was determined not to go back to the way I was and I feel much more confident about myself now,' he continued. 'Exercise, sex and chocolate are great for making you feel good and I am doing two out of the three! I train for about an hour five days a week and feel I'm in the best shape I've ever been. I can eat what I want and that includes scoffing half a big bar of Cadbury's a day.

'I love the fact that I have a six-pack – which I haven't had for years. I'm the same weight I was in the "Mysterious Girl" days, fifteen years ago – I feel more energetic and younger. OK, I'm getting a few lines, but when you get to your mid-30s they start to creep up and you have to let it happen.'

Pete might have been feeling more comfortable about his appearance, but he was increasingly rattled by the numerous rumours that he had already lined up another girlfriend. Indeed, according to some people he'd had a whole series of liaisons, something he totally denied. 'For every person I've been accused of sleeping with, I'd take a lie-detector test. I'd be willing to stand in court and swear on oath it's not true,' he declared. 'There will come a time when I'll be with someone and then I'll be told I was seeing them all along – you just can't win. But I don't have a girlfriend and I haven't slept with anyone. I'm not a prude, but I don't want to rush into bed with just any girl. Yes, I'm a hot-blooded Greek guy and I'm like any other man, but it hasn't been my priority since the split. When you're not with someone, your sex drive disappears but my focus isn't on being with someone else – it's on sorting my life out and moving on. I'm only thirty-six and I've just come out of a bitter divorce battle. I could meet someone today, but I'm not planning it and I feel better about that because it gives me a sense of freedom. I enjoy being single.'

And one factor helping Pete to cope was the children: he had frequently spoken out about how much they all meant to him, and that was now more than ever the case. Determined to do his duty as a father, he could not have come across more warmly on the subject of his offspring if he'd tried, and this applied to Harvey as much as it had ever done. Indeed, Pete sometimes seemed incapable of containing his emotion on the subject of the kids and it was they who had helped him to get through a very difficult time.

'I learned how to become a father before I became a biological dad and that was all thanks to Harvey, or "H", as I love to call him,' he said. 'I've never forgotten those special moments that I spent with him before Junior and Princess came along. He taught me so much and inspired me to write my new single. Now I get to spend every other weekend and certain holidays with him, but I have to respect the fact that he is not my child. As much as I would love to have him more, that is what I am being given permission for. The children have definitely been my lifeline and my focus, and they got me through the divorce. It feels like I've been given a new lease of life. Now I've just got the kids, all of my attention is on them. I'm very firm with them, but not as strict as my parents were with me. I believe in discipline and the naughty step works wonders!'

Pete was also very much aware of the fact that one day, the children might not want to be on his television shows any more. Harvey didn't appear, because Katie wouldn't allow it, but Junior and Princess featured regularly with their father on his various reality shows, and Pete was aware that this might one day change, too. 'There will come a point with the show when maybe we don't want to do it as a family any more,' he said. 'Junior may say, "Dad, I don't like it," then we won't do it. But he is such a star and loves the attention. He loves the ladies, too – I call him JJ Gabor!

'Princess's nickname is Bubbles because she is bubble and squeak – meaning half-Greek! She's the most important girl in my life. I cringe when I watch myself on TV,' he continued. 'I also lack confidence when it comes to asking women out – I can't just go up to a girl. I know it sounds a bit weird, but it's the truth.'

All this seemed to suggest that, finally, matters might be settling down. But the ramifications of Katie's trip to the jungle continued to make themselves felt and there was soon another outbreak of hostilities, although this time not between the key players, Katie and Pete, but between Pete and *This Morning*, his television show. It had become increasingly obvious that he was being put in a very difficult situation, for as showbiz reporter for the programme, he was expected to comment on *I'm A Celebrity...* Indeed, he had even been set to fly out to Australia to do so. Kate's participation clearly made this impossible, but his bosses were furious when he told them that he wouldn't be able to go.

'Pete was really looking forward to going back to the jungle but as soon as he found out that Katie was going to appear, he said there was no chance in hell he would go,' revealed a friend. 'Pete reckons there's no way he could speculate on Katie's antics and any outback flirtations in an unbiased way. *This Morning* executives are livid and have done all they can to change his mind, but Pete refuses to back down.'

Meanwhile, over in Australia, the celebrities were getting ready to strut their stuff. 'You'll see me under the waterfall in my bikini,' declared a cheery Sam Fox. 'I'm proud of my body; I just want to show women in their forties we can still look great. There's a lot more to me than a pair of boobs. You don't survive in this business for 26 years just because you've got a great pair of boobs!' The list of participants had been finalised: along with the previously mentioned celebrities were former *EastEnders* actress Lucy Benjamin, *This Morning* chef Gino D'Acampo, snooker player Jimmy White and actor George Hamilton.

Not everyone was so relaxed about showing off their figures, though. 'I will not be showering naked,' said

Camilla Dallerup. 'I'll find a bikini that doesn't fall down when you're in the shower.' Meanwhile, Justin was thinking about some interior design: 'I imagine we'll be weaving all types of baskets, creating gorgeous throws and blankets from grass,' said Justin. 'I'll be catching wild bees and using honey and wax to make scented candles.'

As for Colin – 'There are loads of rumours that Jordan is going into the jungle,' he confided. 'If she does, and she's looking for a new husband, I might just divorce Justin and marry her. Then I can bring out an album – it will be great!'

There was, of course, one bona fide heartthrob and A-list actor in among them all: George Hamilton. George, a Hollywood star now as famous for his perpetual tan and interesting private life – he had once been married to Alana Stewart and was a long-time friend of Elizabeth Taylor – was something of a curiosity in this company, and if Katie really wanted to put the cat among the pigeons, she could make eyes at him. He did, however, have a girlfriend and, at seventy, was perhaps a little older than she might have been looking for, but his presence contributed to an interesting mix.

George himself appeared to think that his heyday was behind him. 'I know everyone is expecting me to turn up all dashing in a tuxedo,' he said. 'But that's over with. Before I left, I went to a barber and had a $7 military haircut. There's no way I can keep up my usual appearance in the jungle. At home, my hair is woven by angels at night, so I had to have it shaved off. It was cut with a razor and now it looks like it has had Viagra. It is all standing on end.'

The old rogue certainly wasn't completely giving up, however, confiding that what he would really like to take into the jungle with him was a silk robe, a bottle of martini, a stuntman and a make-up man. 'The stunt double can do all the hard stuff and the make-up man can touch me up at the end of the day to make sure I'm looking all right,' he explained.

His fellow contestants had their tales to tell, too. 'I'm not getting out of bed in the dark with spiders dragging my knickers off. I'm going to pee wherever I can,' said Kim, before adding, apropos her co-star Aggie Mackenzie (with whom she was rumoured not to get on and who had appeared on ITV's *Dancing on Ice* the previous year), 'I couldn't be as bad as she was with the skating. I don't think I could eat bugs, and I wouldn't be too keen on crawling around in a dark cave.'

The contestants were quizzed about their phobias: Sabrina Washington's were planes and heights. 'I sleep with my eyes open,' she confided. 'I look like I'm awake, but I'm sleeping. That must be scary for someone sleeping next to me.'

Colin didn't have any phobias, but Justin didn't enjoy

being around creepy crawlies. 'It's like a spa, isn't it?' he observed. 'It's the Skippy Spa, where you eat kangaroo and see the pounds come off – fantastic!'

Gino D'Acampo's phobia was eating bugs, though he had certainly savoured unusual culinary fare before. 'I cooked donkey testicles with sage and butter on Sardinia and they are amazing,' he said. 'It's one of their specialities.'

George Hamilton said he was phobic about everything, and added, 'None of my celebrity friends will be watching. They think I'm on a yacht in the South of France surrounded by beautiful women.'

Sam Fox was none too keen on spiders, snakes and rats. 'I'd love to come home from the jungle and be able to kill a spider,' she said. 'I'd feel really proud of myself.'

Former *Hollyoaks* star Stuart Manning said that he had no phobias, although his fellow celebrities would have something to put up with: 'Everyone will know I sleep well because I snore,' he said. 'I grind my teeth as well, so that's an interesting one.'

Lucy Benjamin didn't like insects and birds, which suggested the jungle could be a bit of an ordeal for her, and on top of that, she was already missing her daughter. 'Three days is the longest I've been away from my daughter and it's her fourth birthday on November 22,' she said. 'It will just be awful.'

As for Jimmy White, he was none too keen on snakes

but he was hoping to lose a bit of weight. 'I've got the Masters coming up in January, so when I come out of the jungle, hopefully I'll be able to fit into my old suits,' he said.

The contestants all had something else to contend with as well: the arrival of Katie, which had still not been officially confirmed. Clearly, the producers were hoping to squeeze the maximum amount of publicity they could out of the appearance by keeping everyone, both in the camp and away from it, speculating for as long as possible, but it was obviously causing trepidation in some quarters. 'I'm scared of Katie Price because she can be a handful,' Camilla rather unwisely admitted, given that Katie was practically on her way. 'I was very much Team Pete.'

Lucy also felt that a jungle with Katie in it could be scary. 'It will be interesting to get to know her if she does land in the jungle,' she observed. 'She's a tough cookie.'

She was certainly that, but in the run-up to her appearance in the jungle, Katie made an uncharacteristic mistake. She was still trying to crack America – indeed, an onscreen argument with Pete about which one of the pair was better known in the States was said to have been one of the final catalysts leading to the break-up of the marriage – and as such appeared on the *Chelsea Lately* show. But she didn't appear to understand that almost no one in the States knew who she was – and they didn't care, either. For once she became the victim of someone else's sharp tongue, rather than lashing out herself.

'You're a big star in England, right?' Chelsea kicked off. 'Why don't you explain to people in the audience what you do?'

'Well, how long have you got?' was Katie's reply.

'Six minutes,' said a very unimpressed Chelsea.

Katie, perhaps taken aback at the sharp tone of the questioning, came out with a few mutterings about family and underwear, but she didn't impress. Nor did she manage to explain what she actually did. Then the subject of Alex came up: 'I don't know if it's big here,' she replied. 'He does cage fighting, UFC, do you have it over here?' In actual fact, cage fighting was hugely popular in the States and Katie's complete lack of understanding of her host country was not going down well.

'Maybe,' Chelsea replied rather coolly, before continuing, 'So, is he a celebrity too now then?'

'He might be now he's pictured with me everywhere,' Katie unwisely replied.

'Well, you're obviously going to take him straight to the... middle,' countered an increasingly sharp-tongued Chelsea.

The subject then turned to Katie's penchant for cosmetic treatments, clearly something she felt more comfortable with, although this would not be enough to pacify Chelsea, who seemed increasingly short with her guest. 'I always fly over here to get my Botox done – I'm mad, I love it,' Katie enthused. 'I've even got LA boobs. Come to LA and everyone has had it done. I always get my hair extensions done here as well, not that I'm high maintenance or anything.'

'Well, you're really helping our economy,' Chelsea observed drily. 'We could use it.'

The subject turned to why Katie operated under two names, but even here she was not her usual verbose self: 'I use the name Katie Price and Jordan, don't ask me why.'

And Chelsea didn't. 'I'm not going to ask any more,' she explained. 'You can go live with your horses and your kids and get Botox – I don't give a shit!' It was not exactly Katie's finest hour. As for Chelsea herself, it was unclear why she felt so hostile: either she simply took an instant dislike to Katie or she felt resentful about having to have her on the show. Whatever the reason, it did Katie no favours at all.

Meanwhile, *I'm A Celebrity…* was finally kicking off, still without Katie in situ, and hosts Ant and Dec were jovial about it all. 'We think it's a really good line-up,' said Dec. 'There are surprises in store. We can't wait!'

The Bushtucker Trials began: although Katie was to have her fair share of them when she finally made it into the show, for now it was her fellow contestants who had to suffer the gruesome tasks they were set to perform. Sam Fox was forced to keep a water spider in her mouth for 30 seconds before fighting off crabs, eels, Australian insects called yabbies and beach worms. Gino D'Acampo was also taking part and informed Sam she was his 'sexual inspiration' when he was younger: in reward, she sang 'Touch Me', her 1980s' hit. Then he, too, had to hold a spider in his mouth, but the duo were thrilled when they managed to win nine out of a possible eleven stars. Lucy Benjamin then had to tackle a 12,000-ft parachute jump.

Only now, when everyone else was firmly in place, was it finally and officially confirmed that Katie Price would be going into the jungle, too. She was hoping to enjoy a repeat of her hugely successful stint in 2004: 'I'm going back in because it's an amazing experience and I want closure on the fairytale,' she commented.

But from the outset others realised that Katie should expect very different treatment from before. 'Katie will not be given an easy ride into the jungle,' warned an insider, and how right he turned out to be. *I'm A Celebrity...* producers have a history of putting latecomers through their paces to earn their place in the celebrity camp.

'Remember how Christopher Biggins and Dean Gaffney both had to do live trials? And then Timmy Mallett and David Van Day were kidnapped and forced to spend the night in a jail? Katie will face the same kind of ordeal.'

What he didn't mention, though, was what would prove to be the biggest challenge of all: the public. An awful lot of people out there were still angry about the way Katie was perceived to have treated Pete and the fact that she was already in another relationship: this was to be their chance to punish her – and so they did.

Meanwhile, Katie, blithely unaware of what she was letting herself in for, seemed as chipper as she had ever done. 'On the back of my shirt last time was Jordan,' she announced. 'On the back of it this time is Katie. Why am I doing this again? Because I've got "mad" written across my forehead! For the other people going in there, it's a game show. For me, it's closure: I'm going back into a place where a big fairytale began. I met my husband, I had two more beautiful children from that experience and six years on, I've been married, had the kids, divorced, ready to go back in.'

Pete continued to be unimpressed. He didn't comment publicly, but let it be known how he felt: 'He feels that she is trying to win back the public's affections after a series of PR disasters and she will talk about their kids and their relationship to the entire nation again,' said a friend.

Katie did, at least, say that this time around she certainly wouldn't be looking for love. She might have used the whole experience to keep Alex on his toes, but she had been flirting a little bit too much in the wake of the divorce and now she finally seemed to realise this is not what the public wanted to see.

'I'm not going in there to look for romance,' she stated. 'I'm not in it to win it – I didn't win it last time. I wouldn't like to be the first out: I just want to really enjoy it. I'm doing it for the experience again. We're all stripped down to bare necessities, we are what we are; we've just got to support each other as a team. There should be no egos of who's who in there, we should just stick together and enjoy.'

But anyone who might have thought that she was calming down with age was to be disappointed. 'I'm sure I'll clash with someone,' Katie continued brightly. 'Half of us probably haven't got anything in common, but that's what makes it interesting. If I see anyone argue, I don't want to get involved but I'll say, "Come on guys, just get on!" I don't want to argue with anyone. I'm just going to be myself, and survive it and be strong. At the end of the day, all my fans are brilliant to me. If they're a fan, they're always a fan – and if they're not, they're not.'

But she was more than a little peeved at the current perception of her, as she couldn't help but make clear. 'People at the moment think I'm breaking down: I've lost the plot, I'm not a good mum, I'm a man eater,' she continued. 'They've got all these perceptions, but I think that when people see me again like last time, they'll see I'm grounded, if not more grounded: I'm a lot more mature this time, I've got nothing to prove. I think people will see the real me.'

Katie was actually to find that the public were far more unforgiving than she thought, but she still sounded remarkably chirpy about it all at the outset. Her luxury was to be a picture of her three children: 'I'm going to find it really hard to be away from the kids, but I'm a working mum,' she said. 'I've got wristbands from the kids. They've all made me bands, and they'll just be watching me on telly and be proud of their mum. People will see I love my children. I'm down-to-earth. They'll see I'm nowhere near a breakdown, I'm not nuts – I'm quite normal.'

Of course, she had been in the jungle once before already, and so she knew exactly how hard it would be. She just didn't understand that of all the camp mates, she would be the one who had to take almost the entire burden of the gruesome tasks on offer once she actually went in. 'You can't have an agenda in there,' she declared. 'At the end of the day, you're going to starve, you're going to be bored and there's going to be people you don't like and you don't get on with. You're going to be tired, you're going to get cold. On the other hand, you get to think a lot. You do adapt – you have to keep that fire going.'

And Katie even said that she was prepared to look less than her usually groomed self so that people could see who she really was. On her previous appearance, she went to some pains to ensure her hair was done in a style that would last through the heat and humidity of the jungle, but this time round she had made no such plans.

'The reason my hair was braided last time is that my hair is quite wild and it goes curly, so I put it in braids,' she said. 'So, this time I'm going in with extensions and they'll probably come out in a big knot – a disaster. I'm going to wash my extensions in the river water and they'll matt together and I'll look real grunge. I don't care if I don't have make-up on. I do think the public will vote for me to do the worse challenges ever. Hopefully, I can offer love and support to everyone in there and just enjoy the whole experience.' She was spot-on about the public vote – but whether she enjoyed the experience was quite another matter.

And so she went in, on 15 November 2009. An early indication that her appearance would not go entirely to plan, however, came from the usually affable Ant and Dec: 'I'm sick of hearing about her,' Ant told Dec, as he declared his support for Pete. 'Can we just have five minutes where we don't mention Katie Price? It's not easy for Peter – he's back home with the kids.'

Katie made her entrance quite literally with a splash – wearing a leopard print swimsuit, she dived straight into a swamp full of cockroaches and fish guts. It was an early indication of how she would spend a great deal of her time inside the jungle. For a start she was afraid of water, and this wasn't exactly appealing water, but still she showed that she was nothing if not game. She knew it was going to be hard, too. 'I'm walking through here and it is bringing back memories, but it's where my fairytale started and it's where it ends,' she said rather sadly. 'I knew there was no way they were going to let me just walk into camp, I just knew there was going to be some kind of challenge.' And as for the other contestants: 'They'll love me... maybe.'

Truth be told, this was a moot point. It wasn't just Ant who was wondering whether it really was such a good idea for Katie to return to the jungle: Colin was also doubtful as to why she was there. After all, she'd done it once already, on top of which she'd had to leave her children to join in: 'It's kind of odd,' he observed. 'Why would someone want to come back? I'd say to Dorothy if she wanted to go back to Oz, I'd say, "Maybe it's a backward step, maybe there are other things you should be doing."'

Meanwhile, Gino announced that he'd rather be sharing the jungle with Pete. Sam described Katie as 'pleasant'. Stuart muttered that he was drunk when he'd met her previously, although that didn't stop Colin: 'Stuart seems to be the only single boy in here, so who knows, by next Christmas he may have an album out,' he commented wryly. So, was the reason for all the sniping the fact that their noses had been put out of joint? To put it bluntly, Katie's arrival had stolen the limelight by already producing far more publicity than the rest of the contestants put together.

Back in the UK, Pete remained unimpressed. 'I was approached by ITV to do the show three months ago, but I said no, straightaway,' he wrote in his column in *New!* magazine. 'For me, it would be like going backwards and I am keen to move forwards. And, more importantly, I can't even begin to contemplate being away from the kids for a month.'

In Australia, however, Katie was still doing her best to get on with the others, offering to go without supper on her first night so that they could have more. 'I'll tell you first, I've eaten,' she said. 'I had a big breakfast. I don't mind you lot having my dinner. I've eaten – you'll be starving. I hope to find some friends in here and just genuinely have a laugh and we've just got to stick together in here.'

Some chance! Kim Woodburn got a eleven out of eleven stars on her first Bushtucker Trial when her challenge was to get into a Perspex box called 'The Tomb for Dreaded Descent', where she was submerged with 800 yabbies and 6,000 cockroaches while trying to get eleven stars out of gold balls. The insects were 'nipping her bosom,' she said, inadvertently revealing some breast as she wiped them away.

'You're all the woman I'll never be and more of a woman than I'll ever have,' declared an admiring Justin. Meanwhile, Katie sat and watched: her ordeal had only just begun.

CHAPTER 4

A NATION'S REVENGE

Katie was absolutely right. There was no way the producers of the show were going to let her into the jungle without making a huge spectacle of it all: they knew that her presence would pull in far more viewers and they wanted to milk it for all it was worth. What they hadn't realised, and despite the fact that Katie had expressed her concerns even before she went in, was quite how much the viewing public was going to take this as an opportunity to punish her for the last few months. In the wake of the break-up, she had gone from hero to zero and like it or not, Pete was seen as the wronged one. And the fact that she was now with Alex only made matters worse.

The first challenge, which involved swimming

beneath two logs filled with fish guts and cockroaches, where she then had to unclip twelve yellow balls attached below the water and throw them into a basket, appeared to go well.

'I knew there was no way they were going to let me just walk into camp,' said Katie. 'I just knew there was going to be some kind of challenge. I'm just pleased I got some balls into the basket, to be honest. I didn't think I'd even get one at the start because I didn't want to get in the water. I'm not really any good with water and I can't tell you how much it stinks!'

Now that she had done well, Katie was allowed to pick seven treats, opting for coffee, tea, chocolate, cordial, salt, milk and sugar. 'They'll love me… maybe,' she said. 'Maybe' was the right word for it: in order to give her fellow celebs the gifts, she would be forced to get rid of the camp's luxury items, a sure ploy on the part of the show's producers. And it worked. 'I'm going to take in the gifts, they're going to like that, but I don't think they're going to love the fact they're going to have to give up their luxury items,' said Katie – and she was right.

'What I'm saying is there's no food there,' said an irritable Sam Fox. 'We really wanted chilli, salt, herbs and pepper. I can do without milk, chocolate, sugar and cordial.'

Katie, however, remained determined to get on with

everyone. She continued to see it as a chance to redeem herself and was still sounding as equable as ever, reasoned and just wanting to give it all a go. 'I'm so chilled I'll go with the flow,' she said. 'I don't care if I don't win. The show's not about me, it's about all of us. We'll get to know your little secrets. I thought I'd actually be really upset because I'm quite a strong person, but coming in here it's quite different, a unique experience, but I'm all right.

'This is luxury, honestly, just to have fun. When I say fun, we all know the trials aren't very nice but after you've done them, you get the adrenaline – like a pat on the back. Until anyone's been in it you can't explain it. It really is a journey and an experience. I said I hope to find some friends and just genuinely have a laugh. We've just got to stick together in here.'

Camilla Dallerup, however, was not enjoying herself. 'I can't sleep properly and can't think properly. My brain's not working,' she said. 'Can you imagine, it's only three days in, what will happen? I'm scared because I don't want to put my health in danger and I can't think straight. I'm just so scared.' And like the considerably tougher Katie, albeit for very different reasons, she would not last the course.

Katie was certainly doing her bit to pull in the viewers, showering in a red frilly number, while several of the other women were also airing their wares. 'I bet guys are in their element, looking at all the eye candy in here!' said Katie.

It was slowly, however, beginning to dawn on her what life was going to be like, second time around in the jungle. She remained as game as ever, but she was beginning to realise that the public had something to say to her – and they were demanding to be heard. 'I feel absolutely gutted that I couldn't get more stars,' she admitted in the wake of the Bushtucker Trial. 'All I remember is I was swimming and I felt I was being dragged under, and they had to pull me out of the water and my legs were numb, and it was as if they were paralysed. I know it's [the fear of water] in my head, but I can't break that barrier. Gutted!' So, why had she been chosen? 'Because they want to see me suffer, obviously,' Katie said.

Something else that she hadn't been expecting was the feeling of déjà vu. Last time around, after all, had seen some pretty momentous changes in her life and the memories of what had happened before kept flooding back. 'I keep expecting Pete to walk past,' she admitted. 'I've been married, had kids, and been divorced. It's all over, the whole circle, and I'm back here. So weird.' And it was about to get a whole lot weirder still.

Back in the UK, meanwhile, Katie was subjected to some strong criticism from a very unexpected quarter – lingerie boss Michelle Mone, who owned the Ultimo brand. Katie had done some work with Michelle in the past, in 2005, but the two women had fallen out (as Michelle tended to do with a fair few of her models, who also included Rod Stewart's wife Penny Lancaster and his ex-wife Rachel Hunter): she chose this moment to go public with some angry accusations about Katie from the time the two of them had worked together. It was clearly timed to ensure that Katie wouldn't win *I'm A Celebrity...* – not that even she herself really thought she was in with a chance.

'I haven't spoken about this, but she makes me sick,' Michelle wrote on her Facebook page, saying that she had dispensed with Katie's services after just five hours. 'Four years ago, one of my junior marketing girls was fitting her. She was so nervous and she made a mistake. Jordan turned round and called her the C-word. That's why she lasted five hours. Jordan has run out of ideas and is scraping the barrel to try to convince all of us again that she is caring and loving. No respect, not a nice person, stay in the jungle and do us all a favour! That's why I have spoken out this time. From a close source, she is apparently being paid £400,000 to try to con us all again. Hope the public won't get taken in by Jordan this time. Her contract with Ultimo was for a year. It lasted five hours. No matter who you are, you should have respect and never speak down to people. As my mum has always taught me, it doesn't matter who you are – rich, poor, famous or the Queen, we are all human beings – so respect is key.'

This certainly wasn't how Michelle was feeling when she hired Katie to represent the 'Young Attitude' brand in 2005, when she declared, 'I am really excited we have signed Katie. Her personality reflects what Young Attitude stands for – sexy, fun and outgoing.'

Nor could Katie respond: she was in the jungle, after all, and so she didn't know what was going on in the outside world. One of her spokesmen spoke out: 'No one in Katie's organisation has any knowledge of these allegations,' he declared.

As for Michelle, she appeared to be having second thoughts: 'I did not write this to get it into the papers,' she said. 'Perhaps I'll need to be more careful in future. The last thing I want is to get that woman any more publicity. These are my views and I just said it like it is.'

Back in the jungle, Michelle was the last thing on Katie's mind. She still appeared to be mourning the end of her relationship with Pete: far from giving her closure, at times Katie seemed to be mourning what she had lost. 'Hopefully he'll watch and realise what a decent person I am,' she said rather sadly. 'The girl he married, not the monster. The weird thing is that the Palazzo Versace hotel where all the contestants stay is about ten minutes from where Pete's family live. I hope they will watch the show too and think, that is the Kate we know.'

It seemed that Pete had been on to something in his cautious attitude towards revisiting the jungle, for Katie certainly didn't look like a woman who was moving on: quite the reverse, in fact.

It was 'love at first sight' when she first saw Pete, she told the other contestants, and in many ways it looked as if that love existed even now.

But Pete was having none of it: the marriage was over and he really did want to move on. 'I will not be watching a minute,' he told a friend, who then continued, 'Peter made it clear he won't tune in. When Jordan was on screen talking about him, he was watching *Toy Story* with their children then tucking them in bed. She is wasting her time trying to win his approval. And as for her looking for closure, Pete already has that and he is moving on.'

Katie, however, didn't seem able to do the same, as became increasingly obvious during the course of a conversation she was having with Colin. 'It's never over because you've got kids,' he told her.

'Too much has happened now,' Katie replied. 'So much damage has been done. I knew before I got on the plane. I saw a picture and I thought, "Wow!" It was instant. He kept getting his kit off and I thought, phwoar! Good old pecs.'

She revisited the theme later in the Bush Telegraph (where the contestants get to air their views to camera):

'Those whole six years have gone so quickly and so much has happened. I'm like, Oh my God, this is a dream! But it's not, it's reality – sad, really.'

This could not have been easy viewing for Alex: after all, Katie was supposed to be with him now. And it was time for another Bushtucker Trial: Katie was picked again, but this time she didn't do so well. She only got four of the twelve stars in 'Deathly Burrows', providing her fellow contestants with a tiny meal of crocodile's feet. First, she had to burrow through a mineshaft, and in each tunnel had to break down more walls: the first shock came when a wall of cockroaches fell on her. But it was the wall of water that really did for her. 'Get me out of here!' she screamed. 'That water reminded me of my accident [when I was a child] and I thought I couldn't breathe.'

In the meantime, Camilla was clearly having an increasingly difficult time. At one stage, she woke Katie to ask for her help and Stuart was becoming increasingly concerned, asking her if she was able to drink water. 'It goes straight through,' said a tremulous Camilla. 'I've never felt this weak – I'm thinking what a hard job it is to get to the shower.' Could it be heat exhaustion and a lack of food? 'It's the not-eating,' Camilla replied. 'I feel useless being here so tired – you can't help anyone.'

In truth, the jungle was beginning to take its toll, even if Katie was the one being subjected to the trials. The producers knew that a combination of heat, hunger and boredom would create plenty of stress in the camp, and so it proved. But there were some positive outcomes, too: Gino D'Acampo, who claimed not to have cried for a decade, was reflecting on the fact that he might well do so when he saw his children. 'Yes, that will be good because I don't often get emotional,' he told Lucy.

Lucy, along with Jimmy, managed to win the camp's first celebrity chest, after pushing a log up a tree to lower a bucket and secure the key to the chest. However, since the contestants answered the question wrongly, they were awarded water pistols rather than ice-lollies. There would also be a live trial that night, entitled 'Jungle School', in which a celebrity, to be chosen by the viewers, would have to tackle their worst nightmare. Already, it was looking increasingly obvious who that might be.

Sometimes it was easy to forget there were other people in the jungle, too. Gorgeous George appeared to be enjoying himself: 'George just lays there and delegates while sunbathing,' said Lucy.

George himself was thoroughly gracious about it all: 'They're so kind to me,' he said. 'I don't know if they think I'm so frail that they'd better help me. The trick is to get as many people to do your washing as you can.'

The attention, however, then shifted very dramatically elsewhere. Camilla appeared to be increasingly unhappy, her health was suffering and, she said, the atmosphere in the camp had changed dramatically after Katie's arrival. The resident celebrities, just as much as the rest of the country, seemed to be rooting for one half of the estranged couple or the other. Matters finally came to a head and Camilla quit the camp, not least because there were fears that she might make herself seriously ill if she stayed, but she was clearly enormously relieved to be out.

And Katie did seem to have been an element in her decision to quit. 'I was scared [to speak my mind],' said Camilla, once she was out. 'I knew she [Katie] could be a handful and I was always more Team Peter.'

Kim felt the same and had told Katie she was, 'an attention-seeker who was just after headlines.' 'I am glad Kim has said something. Well done!' Camilla declared. 'I think the problem is some of the celebrities in there are scared to voice their opinions about her.'

Of course, other problems had driven Camilla out, too. As a professional dancer, she followed a regime of regular small meals and she believed the lack of these was making her ill. 'I've decided to leave the camp,' she told the Bush Telegraph. 'I've had a chat with the medics and I've taken the decision because if I stayed any longer, I could risk my health. I have no energy at all. I can't really think straight, it's horrible. I've never had to quit anything in my life ever before.'

She was clearly very distressed, returning to the subject once she'd got out of the camp, as well. 'I can't believe what's gone on,' she continued. 'I've never had to quit anything in my life. I'm a fighter: I work hard and I don't whinge, I get on with things. Unfortunately, I had to quit because I had no energy because I had no fat deposit on me. Once you start to lose weight, you normally start to feed on your fat, but I haven't got anything extra. Today, I felt so weak I could hardly take ten steps. My lowest moment in the camp was when I realised that there was something wrong and my body wasn't functioning properly. It started to affect how I was speaking and my memory, and I've never been so frightened in my life.'

She also explained that she'd asked the producers if she could have some small portions of fruit throughout the day to keep her going, but this had been denied her. It was hardly surprising, however: if they'd started to make exceptions, then everyone would ask for more. The situation was getting to them all – Lucy burst into tears when her luxury, a picture of her family, was taken away.

But one person was feeling the strain more than most. Time for another Bushtucker Trial and Katie was on the line yet again: on this occasion she was forced to stand in a specially-made 6ft-tall wine bottle as bugs were thrown into the opening – insult was added to injury when Ant McPartlin cracked open a real bottle of champagne as he celebrated turning thirty-four.

And it wasn't just the viewers who had it in for Katie: she hadn't endeared herself to her fellow contestants either. The comment from Kim so warmly applauded by Camilla was actually prompted by Katie herself when, a little unwisely, she asked her fellow celebs what they thought of her. Of course, this was a rather self-obsessed question to pose and Kim didn't hold back.

It all started gently enough, with Gino saying (jokingly), 'I thought you would be a right bitch.'

But then Kim got stuck in. At 67, she was more than thirty years older than Katie, and so clearly wasn't frightened of her in the way that some of the younger women could be.

'You are what I thought you'd be… you're a publicity seeker,' she observed. 'You live and die for publicity, and you do it well. As Shakespeare once said, "We fear you protesteth [sic] too much." You said you escaped to come in here, but you've got 12 million people watching you every night. I don't get that. What I'm saying is you do publicity very well and you protest all the time but love it: you live it and dream it.'

Katie, rather taken aback, objected: 'No, I *used* to love it.'

But Kim wasn't having any of it. 'Katie, please, I'm too old for this,' she went on. 'You're standing there

Katie and Alex's marriage in Las Vegas surprised everyone – the happy couple shopped for rings before their ceremony at the Little White Chapel and celebrations at the Spearmint Rhino and Sapphire clubs.

Above: In July 2009, Katie gave a revealing interview to Piers Morgan, speaking about the break-up of her marriage.

© *ITV/Rex Features*

Below: Katie and Alex on holiday in August 2009, soon after news of their relationship was made public.

© *Rex Features*

Above: Alex soon became an important part of Katie's life, joining in with the filming of her TV series.

Below: The couple's relationship continued to make headlines, with photographers following them everywhere they went.

Above left: Finding some quiet time – Katie and Alex relax in the park in August 2009.

Above right: Out and about in Brighton.

Below: Katie and Alex are clearly devoted to each other – here, they steal a kiss while watching a polo match in Spain.

© *Rex Features*

Above left: Alex has always enjoyed spending time with Katie and the children – here, the couple are on a shopping trip with Junior and Princess Tiaamii.

Above right: Keeping fit is important to both Katie and Alex and they can often be seen running together.

© *Rex Features*

Below: Alex is keen to support Katie in whatever she does, and in September 2009 he accompanied her to the Burghley Horse Trials where she was unveiling her latest range of equestrian clothing and equipment.

© *Terry Harris/Geoffrey Robinson/Rex Features*

Above left: Katie is just as supportive of Alex – here, the couple celebrate his cage fight victory in September 2009.

© *Rotello/Rex Features*

Above right: Running in a 10k event for Cancer Research UK.

© *James Cook/Rex Features*

Below: Katie and Alex show their outrageous side while promoting Katie's new book. Alex joined dressage trainer Andrew Gould, Katie's brother Daniel and Phill Turner in dressing up as drag queens for the occasion.

© *David Fisher/Rex Features*

Above: Katie looking gorgeously glam as she arrives at a book signing, with Junior and Princess Tiaamii alongside her.

Below left: Alex is all smiles as he supports Katie on her publicity tour in November 2009.
© *Geoffrey Robinson/Geoffrey Swaine/Rex Features*

Below right: Alex is always in demand as a successful cage fighter. Here, he is pictured during a martial arts class with UFC legend Randy Couture.
© *Jonathan Hordle/Rex Features*

In November 2009, Katie went back into the jungle to appear on *I'm a Celebrity – Get Me Out of Here!* for the second time. She left after a week, after the public repeatedly voted for her to face the famous 'bushtucker trials'.

© *ITV/Rex Features*

because you've got a gorgeous body. You complain, but you wouldn't have it any other way, darling.'

It was, 'all she had known' since she was seventeen, protested Katie.

'I don't mind that, darling, but don't pretend,' said Kim. 'Make as much money as you can. You've got a lovely body but don't pretend that you hate it. You love it, dear. You came from the shower the other day and, as a woman of sixty-seven, I thought, grow up. You know you've got a gorgeous body, you know the men love it, knowing it's all over the papers. You could dip yourself in the pond just as well.'

So, was Kim now going too far? From the expressions on the other contestants' faces she might well have been, but once started, she wasn't going to stop. 'You love it, darling, and I don't blame you,' she continued. 'For some reason you fascinate the papers. Go for it as long as you can, but don't pretend you're not causing a lot of it, please: because you cause it all. And that's telling you straight. You know, madam, that you'll be all over the papers every day. Now stop it, stop your nonsense!' Finally, she calmed down a little, telling Katie to keep going because she 'had something' others didn't.

It wasn't often that anyone stood up to Katie like that, but she took it pretty well: 'We're all talented in our own way, Kim,' she said. 'I've got to laugh out loud to myself. I'm agreeing with you, Kim.'

With that, she was off to the fake bottle Bushtucker Trial, in the course of which Katie proved that whatever else anyone might say about her, she was a good sport. She won six stars after answering questions while lying in a giant bottle crawling with bugs and amazed the other contestants when she returned to camp by sticking a cockroach in her mouth, then spitting it out.

'She's so hardcore,' Lucy observed. True it might be, but even Katie would soon start to feel she'd had enough.

The departure of Camilla had left a gap: it was filled by the amiable figure of the retired boxer Joe Bugner, who provided a much-needed diversion for the celebs. Meanwhile, Camilla herself was delivering a verdict on the celebrities she'd left behind: of George, saying, 'He's amazing. All the girls in the camp fell in love with him.'

Stuart was, 'the camping expert', while Sabrina was, 'a beautiful singer.' Kim, she described as a 'stand-up comedian, hilarious.' Of Sam: 'we'll be pals on the outside.' Justin was, 'sweet – he looked after me,' while Colin was, 'quieter than Justin, lovely.'

Lucy was, 'my pee pal! She's hilarious.' Of Gino: 'a genius, and very caring.' On Katie: 'she has a soft, vulnerable side.' (Camilla was clearly in a charitable mood.) And Jimmy? 'I've got a lot of time for him.'

For the first time, however, concerns were being voiced on the outside that Katie was being given far more than her fair share of the Bushtucker Trials and that it was beginning to take its toll. Admittedly, her mother Amy was the one voicing these concerns, but even so, Katie was having a fair old time of it and a vindictiveness had begun to creep into the viewers' attitudes now that was looking more than a little ugly. Whatever Katie might have done, did she really deserve to be picked on like this?

Amy was asked, what about the money Katie was earning? It was far more than the sums awarded to anyone else. 'It doesn't matter about that,' she declared. 'It's for charity that she's gone in there, so obviously she's going to raise money for that as well. The money is immaterial.'

What Amy was more concerned about was that Katie was doing one trial after another. She had just been picked, yet again, for the next one: this time round she had to climb a rock while poking her hand into dark holes filled with insects, spiders and snakes. 'It goes back to the process of "Let's stone them, let's make them suffer like the gladiators,"' said Amy, and she had a point. For three nights in a row now, Katie had been picked: 'I think the public want to give me a bad time,' she stated simply, and she was clearly beginning to have had enough. Katie was a tough woman, no doubt about that, but she had visibly trembled in the course of some of the trials and the treatment meted out to her was verging on the sadistic: surely, it wasn't benefiting anyone to see her vilified like this?

It was on the verge of becoming counter-productive, as well. Camilla had already walked out for different reasons, and Katie was beginning to feel so fed up that she contemplated doing the same. 'I'm absolutely ready to leave camp,' she admitted. 'I've had enough. I miss my children, I'm hungry – I want a nice bed, and I don't want to have to put myself through these horrible challenges. I don't like it.' Who could blame her? And surely pushing her so far that she eventually couldn't stand it and threatened to leave the camp altogether was going too far?

But public opinion remained firmly on the side of Pete. On Facebook, two pages had been set up in support of Team Katie and Team Pete: while Katie boasted nearly 2,000, Pete had clocked up 97,015 followers. 'Wow! Eat that, Katie Price!' was one of the messages on Pete's page.

'What goes around comes around,' said someone else. 'So enjoyed last night, haven't laughed so much. Let her get all the tasks, then when it's time to vote the first person off, let it be her!'

And there was a great deal more along those lines. What kind of a mother was she, who would leave her children to go into the jungle? Another said there was no way Katie would be getting any kind of sympathy vote. But the public was pushing too hard now and they were also depriving the other contestants of the chance to show what they were made of, too.

The former BBC royal correspondent Jennie Bond had been in the jungle when Katie first ventured there, over five years previously and she, too, had spotted the direction in which the programme might go. 'It's turning into the Katie Price show, isn't it?' she said. 'When you go into the jungle, you really want to do a trial because it's so boring and you want to test yourself. At the moment, with Katie doing all the trials, I feel really sorry for the others. They must be bored stupid but sadly I don't think this is going to end any time soon. Viewers are going to keep on voting for her.' She was right – unless, of course, Katie decided that she really had had enough and walked out.

In the event, Katie picked up nine stars for 'Jungle School': 'I'm really happy with what I've got, but I'm absolutely ready to leave camp,' she insisted. 'I've had enough. I miss my children, I'm hungry, I want a nice bed and I don't want to have to put myself through these horrible challenges. I don't like it.' She was rewarded for this by being picked for the fourth trial, 'Hell Holes Extreme', at which point she really looked as if she was ready to walk. 'Oh please, please, I can't do it anymore,' she told Ant and Dec. 'Can you believe that! Why do they keep voting for me?'

Indeed, the strain was now showing loud and clear. 'I don't need it,' she said, in the wake of the third trial. 'I started panicking, thinking it's going to be me. I was thinking "Not again" because it's live and the pressure. I think the public want to give me a bad time. You can't take it personally, though it's hard not to. They've seen me battered for the last three or four days. Let someone else have a go.'

Amy felt the same way. It was hard to watch her daughter being so publicly vilified, but she had foreseen just such a problem: 'It's painful, but we told her, "You know you're going to get every trial." They're taking their spite out on her. It's like the Gladiators. It's like, "let's stone them,"' Amy insisted once again.

Katie's brother Danny was more positive: 'She loves going into the jungle, she loves the challenges,' he said. 'I don't think it's a bad thing for her, but the trials are mentally very, very tough.'

He was right there, but the trials were not the only thing Katie had to deal with. There was the fact that she still appeared to have feelings for Pete. Asked if she would like to be friends with her ex, she could hardly contain herself: 'I'd love that,' she said. 'If I had it my way I'd still have Pete, eventually, when he comes round, to come up, you know, when the kids have birthday parties, [for] us both [to] be there. It's nice for the kids to have both their parents and both get on.' But Pete wasn't playing ball: Katie might want more contact, but he certainly didn't.

Kim was now the one appearing to be overly

aggressive. Having had a go at Katie, she now rounded on Justin and suggested he get rid of his facial moles: 'Why don't you cut them off?' she asked. 'Those lumps you have on your face. You're a good-looking guy.'

But Justin was no pushover himself. He clearly did not appreciate this line of questioning, and made no bones about it, too. 'I couldn't get rid of them,' he said, and he looked pretty offended. 'They're my character, I love them – that's like saying, why don't you get one of your boobies cut off? Kim, that's quite rude to suggest that I should just cut myself up so I should look better for you. I like to think I get by.'

'You do get by, dear, but why would you have them when you could have smooth skin?' was Kim's reply.

Later she was totally unrepentant. 'He was born with these white moles,' she told the Bush Telegraph. 'Nothing wrong with them, but he loves his appearance. I said to him, "Why don't you get those moles [taken] off?" I thought, OK, I've done a boo-boo.'

Of course, the producers were delighted: this made for great telly, all knockabout stuff. To increase the tensions, they now divided the group into two camps, with some contestants forced to sleep on the floor. Colin picked his team of Justin, Sabrina, Katie, Joe and Jimmy, and they were to stay at the normal camp in relative luxury, while Lucy Benjamin accompanied Gino, Sam, Stuart, George and Kim into grubby Camp Exile, with only one log to sit on and one bed. There was also no shower and only beans and rice to eat. When the celebrities won stars, the food would first go to Base Camp, and it was only after they had been fed that the Exiles would be allowed anything themselves. It was psychological torture of sorts, designed to extract the maximum amount of tension it could.

Meanwhile, life went on. Sam, who lived in a lesbian relationship, surprised everyone when she expressed a desire for a baby.

'I'm going to really try in the New Year,' she admitted.

'I think you should, you'd absolutely love it,' said Katie.

'I really miss the children I never had,' added Justin.

So, would he adopt? Justin and Colin's frequent travels would appear to rule that out.

In the meantime, with boredom rampant, everyone was also becoming obsessed with their lavatorial experiences. 'It's like the worse public lavatory that hasn't been cleaned for 100 years that you have ever experienced in your life,' declared Lucy.

'Someone keeps going in there and keeping the seat up,' added Stuart. 'Someone peed on the seat as well, which is really annoying me.'

'When I sat on the toilet all the backs of my legs were wet. I had someone else's wee on my legs and I had to rub it with a towel,' Lucy inelegantly revealed.

Clearly, everyone needed a break.

CHAPTER 5

PATIENCE WEARS THIN

It was time for 'Hell Hole Extreme' and yet again, Katie proved herself to be a trooper extraordinaire. After making her way up a 60ft climbing wall, dipping her hands into random holes filled with all kinds of unpleasantness, she won nine stars.

But she certainly wasn't having much fun: 'I can't do it. I've had enough,' she insisted, on learning she'd been picked for the trial. 'Can you believe that? I'm so drained from it, I don't know if I've got the energy to do it any more. I've had enough of it, the torture. I feel like I'm being executed every day. How much more can a person take? People have seen me do it now. Let someone else have a go.'

But the nation loved it. *I'm A Celebrity...* was pulling

in an average of 8 million viewers, sometimes nearly 9 million, every single one of whom appeared to be enjoying watching Katie suffer but Pete was definitely not among their number. 'I know a lot of you have asked me about my thoughts on *I'm A Celeb*, but unfortunately this year I haven't seen it. I do love the show, but once kids in bed I hit the gym (at home),' he wrote on his Twitter page. Beyond that he just would not be drawn.

Back in the jungle, Katie was still sounding philosophical about it all. Chatting to Ant and Dec after the latest Bushtucker Trial, she knew exactly why she was being picked to do every task. 'Probably because I'm the baddie, apparently, as people think,' she said. 'But I am a good person and I love it in camp because the more I get to know them, the more banter and cheerier I'm getting. I know I'm not a bad person. I'm a bit pissed off, to be honest – just how much more can a person take? People have seen me do it now. Let someone else have a go.'

Meanwhile, Gino was creating a bit of controversy on his own. He killed and cooked a rat for his fellow inhabitants in Camp Exile: 'We need protein,' he explained. Eventually the others all agreed to eat a bit, and discovered that they enjoyed it: 'It was actually quite nice,' George admitted. 'We all said it was like chicken but chickeny-beefy kind of stuff, so it was actually very nice. If you kill it, you should eat it.'

'It was better than the crocodile foot we ate, so I think if I had to choose between the two I'd have rat again,' Lucy chipped in. In actual fact, this would go on to create quite a stir.

But Katie's plight was also continuing to cause concern, even among the television professionals, who now realised there was a real chance that she'd leave the camp if she kept on being picked for every single Bushtucker Trial. Those old troopers Ant and Dec also understood as much and appeared to be trying to warn the viewers that their actions might backfire, to say nothing of the fact that they were not allowing the other celebs to do their stuff: 'It's a shame she keeps getting chosen to do the trials. I want someone else to do them,' said Ant.

'She's beginning to crack,' observed Dec. 'She's really upset now. But it's never going to change – she's always going to do them.'

And he was right. To her despair, Katie was picked for the fifth trial: 'Oh, you're joking,' she said. 'Someone else, please.' For once she would not be doing the trial alone, though, as Kim would be joining her (the public, having witnessed the spat between the two, certainly had a sense of humour). Even so, Katie looked close to tears.

Lucy, however, was not in a sympathetic mood. 'I think Katie loves the attention,' she said. 'That's what she's about: she's an exhibitionist. She likes standing there in her little see-through knickers and stuff. She's all right, she can handle it.'

Admittedly, Katie loved all the attention, there was no doubt about that, but this was quite a different kind. Over and over she was tormented, and the torture was both mental and physical: physical for obvious reasons and mental because she knew that everyone wanted to watch her suffering, too. And there was no let-up in sight. She may have been bantering with her team mates, but the public still had an appetite for a great deal more punishment: Katie was nowhere near out of the woods.

The atmosphere of mutiny appeared to be spreading, too. The latest contestant to threaten to walk was Gino: 'I didn't give my all to the endurance test because I thought the game was silly,' he said. 'I thought we would have to use our brains under pressure and I thought we would be pushing ourselves – I never thought I would come into the jungle and hold a stick connected to a bucket.'

Tensions were certainly beginning to rise to the surface. Joe and Justin had words, when Joe accused Justin of allowing other members of the camp to help him prepare dinner and thus allowed it to be burned: 'You've only been here a day and a half, and you are already upsetting people,' Justin snapped in return. Sabrina was also getting a little snappy, but still the attention continued to focus on Katie, who was now preparing for her next trial.

This was to be an *I'm A Celebrity...* special, in which Katie and Kim would be forced to eat any manner of disgusting things. Katie managed a cockroach and a fish eye, but drew the line at a kangaroo's testicle: 'I've been known for eating stuff, but I'm not going to be known for eating a testicle,' she said. 'I can't even go there. I'm passing on them.'

Kim, however, managed it: 'This is ghastly,' she said, barely able to keep it all down.

The food was dispensed via the 'Vile Vending Machine': 'Koala Balls', 'Saltesers', 'Chewing Bum' and 'Twixety Grub' were just some of the delightfully-named delicacies on offer: Katie won three stars and Kim got five.

Kim was not amused: 'I'm appalled of East Sussex,' she told Ant and Dec. 'A woman of my position doing these things. You're ratbags! I'll never watch another show of yours. If you were gentlemen you'd go in there and eat it yourself.' No chance of that.

Although Katie had frequently mentioned her past appearance on the programme, not least it being the occasion when she met Pete, she had avoided talking too much about the break-up itself. Now, however, she began to do so. He was a huge part of her life, of course, and everything was still very fresh: it was hardly surprising that her feelings started to pour out now. 'It's so sad,' she said. 'When you split up with someone, it's not just them you leave, it's the family.' But of course, it had been Pete who left her, not the other way round. Katie appeared to be pining for him as much as ever – although, of course, Alex was now waiting for her on the outside.

Camilla was also outside now, and beginning to take a different line about Katie. Katie had, after all, been very sympathetic and helpful when Camilla started to have a funny turn, and Camilla appreciated it, too. 'I know everyone is calling it The Katie Price Show, but we are seeing a completely different side,' she said. 'She was so nice and helped me when I needed it – I don't know what I would have done without her. I had a couple of nights with no sleep because I was under a berry tree, which kept dropping its fruit like bullets. I also had the smoke from the fire in my face. I went into the booth to talk to the producer. I was feeling so unwell that all I could do was cry, which is hideous because I hate whingeing in the first place.'

Camilla revealed what the rest of the camp felt when they learned that Katie was about to appear. 'We talked about Katie before she came in,' she recalled. 'We decided that given everything that was in the press, we would just try to welcome her. We said, "She's a human being like the rest of us and we only know her from what we read in the papers. Let's just see what she's like." She was very sweet to me. She could tell that I wasn't feeling very well and said to me, "Listen, I'm a mum and I know what it's like. I can wake up in the night, no problem, because my children wake too. So if you feel unwell, just wake me.'

Indeed, Camilla was sounding warmer and warmer still. Not only had Katie made an effort to be nice to her, but she had done so while she was still exhausted and struggling with the shock of arriving in the camp. 'Katie was jet-lagged,' she went on. 'She'd just arrived, just met me and she didn't have to be nice. I actually did go and wake her in the night because I felt very unwell, and she got out of bed and went to the doctor with me. We really saw a new side to Katie – a lovely, lovely girl; a woman who's a mother and who cares for people. But I think sometimes she puts on a brave face, the Jordan brave face without tears, but she's such a vulnerable girl underneath.'

As for the whole jungle experience, Camilla was adamant not all of it had been bad. 'We had so much laughter,' she recalled. 'It was a riot, but you didn't see any of this. It's sad you didn't get to see how much fun I had as well. All you got to see was someone who had gone into shock. I loved it. I got to meet some amazing people and I would have gone on, had it not been for the medical advice to leave.'

Katie was certainly being portrayed in a different light. But the public still wasn't having any of it: they were still determined that as long as she was in that jungle, they would make her pay for her various failings, something which, unsurprisingly, was on the verge of causing Katie to snap. It was a wonder she'd ever managed to get over her jet lag, because she had just been called upon to complete a sixth Bushtucker Trial, 'Car-lamity', which she did, winning eleven stars out of twelve. She had to drive a mini-Jeep around a specially designed course, which was filled with items such as a drive-through restaurant, which served bugs. She didn't look very enthusiastic: 'I just want to go home,' she told Ant and Dec. 'I'm so unenthusiastic today, it's like how much more can a girl possibly do? I want to go. Is there any way I can get out? I would love to be the one going out. This is mental torture now, what the public are doing to me. Am I loved or hated? I don't know. If I walk out, then I don't need the money. Others in there do. I don't. I've got money – I have just done a big book tour. This isn't about the money, anyway.'

In the event, she had to stop at four locations on the way to find stars: a tank filled with jungle goo and three stars, then the drive-through, where she had to eat foods including French flies, a cobweb filled with spiders and stars, and a jungle car wash where she was gunked.

To everyone's surprise, however, not least her own,

Katie thoroughly enjoyed this particular challenge, which she carried off with aplomb. 'That's something I would do with the kids,' she said afterwards, with a broad smile. 'They'd love all this slime. I actually enjoyed that and I'd do that again. Thank you, public, you made me do something fun. I'll be putting my feet up now all afternoon, like a little princess.'

By that time she had well and truly had enough, though. After nearly a week of non-stop Bushtucker Trials, she just couldn't take it any more. The seventh was called 'Bad Pit' and was based on a snake-infested island. The 'Katie' Trials were certainly working wonders with viewing figures: by now about 10 million were tuning in every night. She was now chosen, alongside Joe Bugner, totally overshadowing the fact that Lucy, Sam and Gino had been picked as the first set of celebrities up for potential eviction. 'I'm not doing it,' she declared.

And who could blame her rebellion? Katie had performed above and beyond the limit of human endurance: a lesser woman would have thrown in the towel long before now. But she had performed one trial after another, visibly scared at times, but determined to prove that she was not the bad person that the public thought she was. Enough was enough, however.

One person who definitely felt that it was time to stop picking on Katie was Alex. He was now on his way to

Australia to meet her when she came out and it transpired that his affections had only solidified while his partner went through all that she had endured.

'I'm definitely asking her to marry me and I'm convinced she's going to say yes,' he confided. 'One idea is I make the proposal in front of cameras on the show. But whatever happens, I know this is right. I've never felt this way before and I'm convinced Katie's going to feel the same way. I already have a ring in mind, but I'll have to see what takes my fancy when I go to the jewellers. It will be a ring fit for the princess she is.'

It wasn't entirely clear yet whether Katie felt the same way: indeed, she was to blow hot and cold for quite some time before she finally decided that Alex was the right man for her. However, another marriage was definitely on the agenda: she liked being married and wanted to return to what she'd had before.

'I love that whole family unit. Love it,' she declared. 'Absolutely 1000 per cent, I'd get married again. If I found the right one, I'd do it now. I'm not going to wait. If I find the right one and it feels right, I'm going to marry now. I'm 31, I want to get settled down.' But would it be with Alex? Katie still wasn't sure.

Meanwhile, Katie was certainly having a lot of fun with Colin and Justin, which was hardly surprising as she gets on extremely well with gay men. Apart from anything else, they were the only men who she knew for a fact were not going to leap on her when she wasn't expecting it, and that went down well. The trio joked about redesigning a house for Katie: Justin said he would do her bedroom, adding, 'We would give your bedroom more of you.'

So, would she be a difficult client? asked Colin. 'Oh, no, I'm easy,' Katie insisted. 'I would say to you to do whatever you want. Anything's better than what I've got at the moment. It's a nice house, but there's no style in it at all.'

Two more gay men with whom Katie got on extremely well were her close friends, make-up artist Gary Cockerill and DIY expert Phill Turner, who had just arrived in Australia to greet her when she got out of the jungle. Would she walk out? Not according to Phil: 'Katie is not a quitter,' he said (he was right, but the fact remained that she couldn't take much more). 'You're seeing a genuine girl on that show and we love her. Everyone would be terrified of the trials she's done. She's doing amazingly.'

As to why she was being picked for all the Bushtucker Trials – 'I think everyone is misreading that,' said Gary. 'People want to see Katie doing the trials because she's the most interesting person in there.'

He was right there, although Kim appeared to be trying to put in a rival bid. She managed to pick a row with Joe over cooking dinner, which started when Stuart made an attempt at preparing Australian lamb: 'I think you can handle this very easily,' Joe told him. 'You know, that big, beautiful pan of yours. Fill it nice and hot, plunk a bit of oil in there, your herbs with it.'

'Joe, you do it,' said Kim.

'No, he's got to learn, darling,' Joe replied. 'Leave it to me.'

'No, he doesn't want to learn,' snapped Kim. 'I'd rather you do it, Joe. You've done no cooking – he's done so much. Please cook. Either shut up or do it, but leave that poor man alone!'

At this, Joe told her to calm down, adding, 'Don't you dare speak to me. Don't you dare speak to me like that ever!'

Katie got up to try and calm everyone down, but Kim pushed her away. 'You disgust me,' Kim hissed at Joe. 'You've got to pull yourself together and realise we're a team.'

'You've really embarrassed me, Kim, I thought you were a nice lady,' snapped Joe. 'I think you've got a couple of loose ones.'

In the end they kissed and made up, but that, too, was overshadowed by the fact that finally, Katie really had had enough. She was refusing point blank to do the seventh trial: 'I'm not doing it – sorry, someone else will have to do it,' she insisted. 'I'm not in it to win it. It makes no odds to me, it's not about the money – I didn't come back here for that. I really miss my kids. I've done all my challenges, people can see that I'm genuine – I just don't want to be here anymore.'

In fact, not only would she not do the challenge, she wasn't going to stay in camp, either – this time, she really had had enough. 'If I thought about my reasons for being here, what are they?' she continued. 'A cheque for all of us is always attractive, but it's not as if I can't earn money at home. It's not always about the money: I met a husband here, had kids and I've had so much shit, coming back is like a big circle for me. I didn't break down, I was strong because this is a unique place to meet someone and there are lots of reminders here all the time. I sit there and I picture things. I've done the hardest bit I had to do – constant reminders of the past – but I've dealt with it and been strong. When Pricey makes a decision, she sticks with it. I'm really sorry for letting everyone down, but I can't continue this journey for personal reasons. I'll walk with my head between my toes in shame, and I'll probably regret it. I feel sick for letting people down, I'm gutted myself I'm leaving.' In actual fact, she really didn't have anything to be sorry about: few people could have endured as much she did.

Despite her ordeal, however, and the fact that she was leaving the jungle early, plenty of commentators were adamant she'd done herself no harm at all in appearing on the series once more. She had certainly proved she had guts, and she had not come across as a monster at all: 'By doing six tasks, she's got a huge amount of television time,' Mark Borkowski, PR expert and author of *The Fame Formula*, pointed out. 'It's demonstrated to the audience who she is.'

And so Katie walked, and in so doing managed to cultivate even more publicity, given that she also took the occasion as an opportunity to dump Alex. 'I've done a lot of reflecting and I think that it's best I'm on my own,' she told Ant and Dec. 'I just don't want to be in a relationship, I want to be on my own. I hope we can remain friends.' Asked when the split took place, she responded: 'As of when I came out. I'm not with him now.'

But it had certainly given Katie time for some mature reflection on the events of the past year. After the split from Pete, she really hadn't appeared to be thinking at all: as soon as she'd recovered from the shock (in fact, probably well before then), she simply plunged herself into one attention-seeking activity after another, not least so she wouldn't have to think about what had happened to her marriage to the man she loved. But the public's reaction had brought home to her that this was not the best way to go about a recovery and that, above all else, she should just calm down.

'Maybe they wanted me to suffer,' she told Ant and Dec. 'It was torture. I half-expected it and half not. I knew I'd get some, but didn't think every day. I'm not as strong as I was years ago: I was petrified and scared, I kept thinking, I don't want to do this, but I didn't want to let the team down. I kept saying I can't do anymore, I'm a human being and I can take only so much torture. My mum said, "I don't think people voted because they hate you." Whatever the reason, it wasn't nice. I'm a human being, you can only take so much beating.'

However, she was now a much wiser Katie, one who realised that it was time to take stock. 'But it's made me reflect on the past,' she continued. 'I did act a fool, behaving like I did. I'm going to come out a better person. The last seven months I acted like a right twit and I'm sorry that I've upset people. This is a new start for me. My number one reason for leaving was I missed the kids so much. I'll never, ever leave them again for this long. Also, the whole place reminded me of Pete from the moment I woke up to the moment I went to sleep. Every second it was Pete, Pete, Pete, and although they were amazing, happy memories I had, I'd lie there and think those good memories are way gone. But then I was still there with constant reminders of Pete, Pete, Pete, Pete.'

And she really wanted to see her children now. 'If I had it my way, I'd have my children here,' said Katie. 'All that matters to me is my children, I'm dying to see them and speak to them. I don't want to be here anymore and nobody can change my mind. It's not about the Bushtucker Trials: I've done so much thinking and reflection while I've been in here. I'm 100 per cent not a bad person – I just want to be with my children, they are my life. I've enjoyed being with everyone in the camp. The other celebrities are all winners to me.'

In fact, the other celebrities were a little taken aback by Katie's departure: 'I thought she'd stick with it until she was voted out, or voted Queen of the Jungle,' said Stuart. 'We were all surprised she gave up, so we're all disappointed but that's Katie Price,' added Gino. 'She was looking for an answer in her private life and she found that and decided it was time to go,' Colin chipped in.

Meanwhile, Lucy was voted out, and Joe and Kim signalled their reconciliation by doing a Bushtucker Trial together. No one noticed.

It was unclear what would happen with Alex. Rumours behind the scenes had it that Katie dumped him because he'd sold a story about wanting the two of them to get engaged. The chances were that she'd been so strongly reminded of Pete in the jungle that she couldn't face looking at another man just then. Nor was she in a hurry to leave Australia: in the wake of leaving the jungle, she headed out for some champagne instead. Her great friend Michelle Heaton was also in situ and the two of them were pictured shopping together, but what the future really held next for her was unclear.

Indeed, while Katie may have been in a more reflective phase about her past behaviour, she was in no mood to be gentle with Alex. Far from the heart-warming proposal that he had been planning, Katie was said to be livid with him, not least for talking about her to the press. He managed to persuade him to see her, but the meeting did not go well and ended, apparently, in a row.

'It's fucking over, Alex,' friends said she told him. 'Once I make up my mind, I stick to it – there is no way back. What the fuck are you doing here anyway? You've had a wasted trip. Just fucking leave me alone! You totally ignored my feelings and I cannot forgive you for that.'

At least she agreed to see him, not that it appeared to be doing Alex much good. 'Katie felt she owed it to Alex to hear his side of the story,' said a friend. 'She let him talk, but nothing he said changed her feelings. *I'm A Celebrity* cleared her head and made her realise that the relationship wasn't what she needed. It's tough for Alex to take, but the relationship seems to be over.'

It didn't help that Alex had checked into the Palazzo Versace Hotel. This was not only where Katie was staying, it was where the entire *I'm A Celebrity...* crew stayed when they were in the jungle, and it couldn't help but look as if Alex appeared to be muscling in. 'When she was told Alex was here, let's just say she was not happy,' revealed Sabrina Washington's best friend Katrina Edwards, also in situ. 'The poor woman!'

Meanwhile, Alex's mother Carol was more concerned about her son. Whatever the circumstances, it's always unpleasant to be dumped but when it happens on live television, that's doubly the case. 'I watched the TV last night and it seemed very cruel the way she spoke about Alex,' said Carol. 'He really loved her and gave up a lot for her, and this is how he gets treated by her. All I know is that he is in Australia and his phone is off. He must be upset. I am worried for him.' Nor was she happy that Michelle Heaton appeared to be giving advice: 'It is between the two of them and it's not right that people are wading in and giving their opinion. They should be left to sort it out themselves.' But Katie-bashing was still very much the order of the day. She had been talking about how much she wanted to see her children: in that case why, demanded her critics, was she still in Australia? It was said that she was finding it hard to get a first-class ticket home, but various airlines still had seats available – it was suspected the real reason that Katie remained in situ was that she wanted to do a photoshoot in the grounds of the hotel.

Back in the jungle, life went on as Colin was voted out. The loss of Katie was already being felt: viewing figures had fallen by about 2 million on the back of her departure. Nor would it appear that she was losing a great deal financially, given that she reputedly set to receive £250,000 of her £350,000 fee, following her departure.

Katie still appeared to be feeling the strain: she lashed out at nearby photographers, crying, 'Show me some respect! Keep away from me.' Another series of her reality show, *What Katie Did Next*, was announced: 'Viewers have seen what I went through in the jungle, and now they'll get to find out exactly what happens next,' said Katie, suddenly calming down. 'As ever, there's bound to be lots of drama!'

Finally, she began her return to the UK, while Alex stayed out in Australia to lick his wounds – if, indeed, there were any genuine wounds to lick. He, too, returned to the UK shortly afterwards, amid rumours that he and Katie had already been secretly reconciled and that her fury had done the trick and convinced him to be more discreet from then onwards.

'Alex and Katie saw a £25,000 ring at a jeweller's in Cheltenham recently,' said a source. 'She loved it, even though it was second-hand. Alex took a photo of it and got a friend who makes rings for Premier League footballers to copy it for him for £9,000. He did not have the money, but managed to borrow £6,000 from his family, and the rest he found himself. He must not do a kiss-and-tell and he can only do interviews that she approves. She has made it clear that if he talks without permission again, he is out.'

Indeed, this appeared to be confirmed by Alex, who was photographed waiting to catch a plane from Brisbane: 'I may as well smile now,' he said. 'I am very, very happy.'

And well he might be: Katie had said that one of the reasons she was returning to the jungle was to get some closure on her relationship with Pete and it seemed she had actually managed to do so. When she was in the jungle, there had been suggestions of a reunion, but Pete was so firmly against that idea that no one could have been in any doubt that this was the last thing he wanted, and that included his ex-wife. Pete was adamant that he hadn't even been watching the show while Katie was on it: all that he was concerned about was the children. It was over, and there was no going back.

At long last Katie began to understand the truth of that, too. For months after the split, she had hankered after Pete, but she was not the sort of woman to spend too long eating her heart out over a man she couldn't have. And so she moved on: Pete had left a long time ago and Katie was over it. Time to start making plans with her new man.

CHAPTER 6

IT'S STILL A JUNGLE OUT THERE

Back in the UK, Katie was still besieged by reporters, curious to know what was really going on between her and Alex, although she herself had just wanted to get home to be reunited with her brood. There was still some semblance of interest in *I'm A Celebrity...* with Jennie Bond, who had been in the jungle with Katie the first time around, professing relief that some of the others would now get a look in. 'I haven't missed it,' she said. 'I have been travelling around the country doing *Cash in the Celebrity Attic* and dashing back to see it. It did become like the Katie Price show, although she is very watchable, but now it will be good to see the other contestants get a chance to do the Bushtucker Trials – we all want to see how they do.'

But what was happening with Alex? Publicly, and very possibly privately, they were still apart despite the reports saying they were an item once more. Indeed, Alex was sounding pretty bitter about it all: 'I helped her through everything when she was going through the divorce and now I'm no longer needed,' he was reported to have told a friend. 'I've passed my expiry date. She's treated me like an idiot. She has been nothing more than a heartless bitch. Katie got publicity from me, not the other way round. I was just another pawn in her game. I love Katie and know things about her no one else does. This has been a hard blow for any man to take – and I've taken some. She has no right to tell me what to do. I'm not stalking her: if she wants me out of her life then fine, I'm gone.'

Right from the start, it was clear that this might not be the end at all, though. It did seem as if Katie had simply flown into a rage when she discovered that Alex had been talking to the press and was now taking a far more conciliatory stance. 'I was really falling for the guy and I can't switch off feelings just like that,' she told *Hello!* magazine. 'So I'm not ruling out anything between us. Strangely enough, I feel more hurt from this split right now than I did with Pete because I had known for some time from seeing a marriage counsellor that it probably wouldn't have lasted. At the moment I'm absolutely livid about the whole situation. I'd always told Alex that I didn't want another Pete and Katie relationship. I'd asked him, please, to stay away from the media, and after the first time he gave a story, even though he was saying really lovely stuff, I told him, one more lapse and that would be it between us. I think he's been very naive and that people are taking advantage of him. If things get sorted out, then fabulous. If not, I'll be on my own.'

Almost immediately afterwards came reports that the relationship really was back on. 'Me and Alex have sorted things out and I'm so happy,' Katie told a friend. 'We've both realised there were some people out there trying all they could to split us up and make money out of us. Alex was a bit naive and realises that now. But it won't happen again – I'm going to make sure that I don't let those same bastards wreck things for me and Alex again.'

Alex appeared equally delighted with how it had transpired. Reports had him telling Katie, 'I can't live without you, I want you back.' Fortunately she agreed, with the result that he was looking considerably happier now: 'He's over the moon,' said a friend. 'He's saying Katie's promised to cook him a massive dinner with roast lamb when he gets back to her house on Sunday. He is convinced his relationship with her can now go from strength to strength.'

Even so, it took a little while before it was all officially on again. Katie was pictured breaking down and friends expressed their concern: 'She is constantly in tears and feels very isolated,' revealed one of them. 'She has a lot of friends, but when they leave, there is no one there for her. Katie feels she has nothing to look forward to. Her book tour is over, it seemed the public hated her in the jungle and she is now single.'

Back in the jungle, George became the third person to leave voluntarily and early, not least because he wanted to get back to his girlfriend, Barbara. 'At my age, the time I have with people I care about is important,' he told Kim. 'Barbara is here and we have no time together. I don't see the purpose for me to stay.' This left Kim, Justin and Jimmy in tears, and given that there were actually only five days to the finale – and George was tipped to win – there was another reason, too. He was being kind: he wanted one of the others to win. 'The last thing I wanted was to go one-on-one with people,' he told Ant and Dec. 'I have too much respect for them. I just thought, why don't I leave while I'm on a high? As much as I would like to win, because I'm competitive, I just didn't want to see any of them lose. Sometimes you lose to win.' Was it any wonder he was called Gorgeous George?

Joe Bugner was the next out, not quite so graciously, given that he claimed the show was fixed. Meanwhile, it was the Katie 'n' Pete 'n' Alex show that continued to intrigue: there was much speculation about what Katie would say when Pete hired a pretty 22-year-old called Nita as the children's new nanny and it was generally felt that the appointment would not go down well.

The pair of them did, however, manage to silence hostilities for long enough to sort out arrangements now that Christmas was coming up. Katie would have the children over Christmas itself, while Pete took them for the New Year: 'Both Pete and Kate were desperate to have the children over Christmas,' said a source. 'There's been a lot of to-ing and fro-ing, but in the end Pete said Kate could have them. He knows how much Christmas means to her and didn't want to cause any more upset to the youngsters. But in return, he asked – very politely – if he could give the kids a New Year's Eve they'd never forget and then take them home to Australia. His mum and dad haven't seen Princess and Junior for months and are desperate to see them.

'Things are much more friendly. They can't ignore what's gone before, but they know the children come first. There's no suggestion they'll get back together but they are on the first steps to being friends again.'

That was possibly overstating it: unofficially, Katie and Alex were an item again and tensions were bound to continue with the best will in the world. Such had been the bitterness of the break-up that Katie and Pete couldn't put it all behind them just like that, but the fact that they were prepared to try and get on for the sake of the children was at least a start.

Back in the jungle Sabrina was voted out. In London, Katie was hitting the hotspots, turning up at the Mandarin Oriental on 1 December for the Morgan Awards (as in Piers Morgan), where she was given the Mae West Adding to the Gaiety of the Nations award (this was a spoof of awards ceremonies) before moving on to Mahiki club. There, she confirmed she and Alex were definitely an item: 'I never stopped loving him,' she admitted. 'I don't care what people think: I want to be with Alex. We'll take it slow this time. Fingers crossed it'll work, because I love him.'

On the night of the awards, however, Alex was not around and Katie seemed to return to her former self with a vengeance, knocking back the booze and having a lively chat with *The X Factor*'s Jamie Archer, although nothing untoward occurred. 'Katie turned up determined to have a good time and didn't seem to be missing Alex at all,' revealed a witness to the event. 'She downed drink after drink and made a beeline for Jamie when she saw him. She knew who he was and chatted to him for ages. Before he left, they swapped numbers.'

But Jamie was keen to reassure everyone that they were just friends. 'She came over and said hi, and then asked me to come and have a drink,' he said. 'We got chatting and she said, "Oh, you've got hair like my

Harvey." She was beaming when she was talking about her kids, which was really nice to see. But it seemed like the whole thing in the jungle had upset her because people kept voting to make her do the trials. I felt like she needed a bit of TLC, so I gave her a hug and told her things would be OK. She's obviously an attractive woman, but she's not really my type, to be honest. I didn't flirt with her or see her in a romantic way.'

Kim was out of the jungle now and giving interviews: she was asked if she regretted giving Katie rather a hard time. It seemed she did not. 'No,' she stated. 'It wasn't blunt at all – it was honest. The thing with Katie is that I can't stand bull. She's not twenty, she's thirty-odd and she needs to grow up. She was doing all this: "The minute I get out, I'll be plagued with photographers." Well, I can't take that nonsense. She lives and breathes publicity – it's what drives her, so she should stop bleating on about it because we know it's false.

'She has an extremely good career, but it won't last forever. I reckon she's got, at most, another four or five years. When she is thirty-seven or so, it will be over, and that girl knows it. I can't blame her for it – I'd do it myself if I had her assets.'

But what Katie wanted now was to work out where it was going with Alex. She continued to feel torn, not least because her great friends, Gary and Phil, were not at all sure he was the right man for her. 'Katie has really been through it this year,' said Phil. 'She loved Peter Andre and this divorce has been so hard for her. Katie needs a man around her, she is always telling us that. But Alex is not the one for her – she needs to find someone else. She doesn't care about being the breadwinner, none of that matters to her. She just needs a real man to dominate her, to take control and stand up to her, and look after her. She doesn't need a doormat.

'Katie keeps changing her mind about Alex. She's lonely since splitting up with Pete and I can understand that. But I wish she would find someone else. Katie is one of my closest friends and I will always be here for her, no matter what. Ultimately, I just want her to be happy.'

Phil felt the same way. 'Christmas will be different this year,' he said. 'Pete and Kate are being civil for the children, but I can't see them sitting down for dinner in the same room just yet. It's likely one will have the children on Christmas morning and the other in the afternoon. They both adore the children, that's what is so heartbreaking.' Indeed, although they were trying to get along, the slightest thing appeared to set them off.

Back in the jungle, Gino D'Acampo was crowned king. ITV wasted no time in broadcasting *I'm A Celebrity... Get Me Out Of Here: Coming Out*, which was posted as a highlights package from the series but, as one critic pointed out, it might well have been a bit of a dig at Katie, who featured heavily and not always in the best light. Ant and Dec made the point that three people had left voluntarily, a 'record-breaking' fact, but from then on, Katie dominated the proceedings. There was footage of her being met by her friend Michelle Heaton, who told her that Alex was on his way out to see her: 'Before I see him, I need to see everything,' declared Katie, decamping to her very luxurious hotel bedroom to study the press they had all received (hence her anger later on about the fact that he had been talking to the newspapers).

She then turned her attentions to her fellow contestant Lucy Benjamin, who was showing an alarming disinclination to cash in on her post-jungle fame: 'I know how to make money from the media,' Katie told her. 'I can get you in a daily and in *OK!*' And then, as Alex was said to be in the hotel's foyer: 'What if he comes up to me? That's the money shot.'

It was all pretty upfront stuff, but surely no surprise to anyone who had followed Katie's career: after all, this was what she did to earn a living and it was also far more entertaining by anything similar being done by anyone else. And now that she was back in Britain, she was as much in demand as ever, turning up in an eye-catching pink and black printed silk dress at the British Comedy Awards on 13 December to present the Best Comedy Television Actor award to Simon Bird of Channel 4's *The Inbetweeners* alongside Alan Carr.

The war between Katie and Pete, however, continued. In some circles, there was much rejoicing when it turned out that Pete was due to have an absolutely bumper year: his career certainly hadn't suffered as a result of the split. His album *Revelation* had sold more than 300,000 copies, his tour was a sell-out and he was much sought after for endorsements, all of which were making him a wealthy man. One of the biggest causes of the rows between him and Katie had been about which of them was the more successful: Pete definitely seemed to be holding his own.

'Our forecasts show Pete will earn between £4 million and £5 million next year,' revealed his agent Claire Powell in December 2009. Graham Stokes, owner of Conehead Records, who signed Peter on a £1 million deal was equally delighted: 'We are all absolutely delighted,' he said. 'There is no reason his musical career cannot go from strength to strength. He is a highly-regarded recording artist and will continue to shift sales over the next twelve months.'

The story was the same at HMV: 'His star appears very much in the ascendancy again,' said spokesman Gennaro Castaldo. And Gary Howard of Marshall Arts concert promoters had even more good news, forecasting that Pete would earn £1.4 million from ticket sales: 'To start with, we put on 29 shows but they flew out of the window,' he announced. 'In the end we put on 37 shows and we have filled them all except one. We could have filled 100. In total we have shifted 70,000 tickets at £24 a pop, not to mention all the merchandise sales.

'I had three of the UK's top promoters working on the sales alone. Peter now holds the record for the fastest-selling show at the Indigo club at London's O2 Arena. We filled that in a day, so we put on another show at the Hammersmith Apollo, selling another 3,500 tickets. That's 6,000 tickets in London, not to mention the other sales around the country. Peter could now start to fill arenas, probably in 2011, and we've even had offers to headline some festivals.'

On the perfume front it was good news, too: Pete's was the best-selling ladies' fragrance in 2009, with 'Unconditional'. 'What has happened to Pete over the last eight months has been traumatic, but the business side of things has been amazing,' his agent Claire added. 'People see him as a genuine guy, that is why sales of his records and endorsements have increased tenfold. Only last week Pete signed a deal to work with Coca-Cola.'

With unfortunate timing, there was another outbreak of hostilities as it turned out that Katie was not happy about Pete taking the children to Australia. Pete's father was ill and so he wanted to fly out there: now it appeared he would have to do so alone. 'Pete is devastated that his dad can't come to England, so he has to go there,' said a friend.

Katie herself was livid and had turned to her lawyer, Fiona Shackleton, to stop her former husband from carrying out his plans. 'She is utterly furious at Pete's intentions,' said a source. 'Like any doting mother she wants to see her children on Christmas Day. If Peter had taken them to Australia, she wouldn't have seen them at all over the entire festive period. She decided to get Fiona Shackleton on the case and so far she has been successful.'

According to a friend, Pete was 'gutted' and saying that he'd hoped Katie would be more supportive: 'He believed that Katie would be more understanding. Relations are only set to get worse.'

Nor was that the only bust-up. Katie had embarked on a book signing tour and was not holding back about what she felt about her ex: in an interview at a book signing in Warrington, Cheshire, she told a radio station: 'I'm sorry to disappoint you, but we will never get back together. All Pete had to do was say, "I don't want a bad word said about my ex-wife," but he never did – he let it carry on. So, in my eyes he is evil.'

Not exactly the recipe for family harmony, with the Christmas season looming up ahead.

The warring continued. Pete was pictured in a smooch with designer Linda Barker (not that it looked to be a very serious one – Linda is happily married), while Katie continued with her book tour. Pete was then photographed taking all three children out for a pizza; Katie was said to be still in love with him. But not everyone was on Team Pete: her new friends, Colin and Justin, really were planning to work on the house with her and sounded very positive whenever her name came up: 'Katie first discussed with us working on her house when we were in camp and was in touch this week to finalise a deal after we returned from Australia,' said Justin. 'We grew really close on the show – I think she has a natural affinity with gay men because we don't have an agenda. We've been planning the project in the last few days. Her priorities are her bedroom and the hallway, then hopefully we'll move on to the rest of the house.'

In mid-December it became quite clear that Katie and Alex were an item again. Together, they turned up for the finale of *The X Factor* and although there were some shenanigans outside – Alex leapt out of the car that had brought them to the studio and hid in a nearby McDonald's before entering the building through a side entrance, while Katie wafted through the main foyer – inside, they were indisputably a couple once more. Katie was even sporting a large rock on her engagement finger, although it meant nothing, she said.

'We haven't announced we are back together,' she told

journalists backstage. 'We're seeing how it goes. I don't care what anyone thinks – it's up to me who I go out with. I always wear this ring on my engagement finger – it doesn't mean anything, really.' With that, they were off to Simon Cowell's dressing room so that Katie could introduce her new love to the great man.

Alex was certainly greatly relieved about the way it had all turned out. 'Ever since Katie returned from the jungle, Alex has been at her house to make her work things out with him,' said a friend. 'Dumping him on TV was such a humiliating thing, but he has the hide of a rhino and Katie seems smitten with him. Taking him to *The X Factor* for their first public date proves it.'

Meanwhile, business was booming. In the battle between Katie and Pete, there had been much dark comment about how Katie's recent wild antics had destroyed her reputation and thus her earning potential, but quite the opposite appeared to be the case. Apart from the fact that all she needed to do to make the front pages was to walk out of her house, the string of endorsements that had made her so wealthy were still racking up. The latest deal came with the very upmarket emporium Selfridges, which was paying her £2.2 million to design a range of baby clothes.

'Katie has wanted to design baby clothes for years,' revealed a source. 'She loves being a mum and kitting her own kids out in an assortment of really cute clobber, and has been planning this range for months. Working with a team of designers, she will initially launch KP Baby as a girls' range with loads of bright pinks and fuchsias – her favourite colours. Kate is determined to be really hands-on with the range and will get totally stuck into every aspect of the design process, from sourcing the fabrics to choosing the logos. There will be everything from baby pink hoodies to bright pink combats. Kate is determined to re-brand herself in the wake of her recent troubles. She's excited.'

Meanwhile, her appearance was as much a preoccupation as ever: Katie proved herself to have more of a sense of humour than anyone might have thought when she dressed up as the Sacha Baron Cohen character Bruno for the 'Stars Dress Up' special issue of *Heat* magazine. Like Bruno, she donned a tight pair of yellow shorts-cum-knitted lederhosen, teamed with a yellow pork pie hat, and posed in a field of yellow flowers: 'When *Heat* asked me to be Bruno, I thought it would be a laugh,' she said. 'I had hardly any make-up on for once – although I have got brown stuff all over my face, which I'm not so sure about. I quite like this look, though!'

The extent of Katie's influence and popularity became increasingly apparent when she became central to a storyline in the long-running soap, *Coronation Street*. It involved the character Rosie Webster, the daughter of

Kevin and Sally Webster (played by Helen Flanagan), who decides she wants to become Weatherfield's equivalent of Katie, or rather, her alter ego, Jordan. To achieve this aim, she takes a job as a vodka promotions girl, which involves moving around on roller skates and firing shots from a water pistol. She also has a set of saucy pictures taken, which turn up in the wrong place.

When you are referenced on *Coronation Street*, then you know you really are part of the nation's life: 'This is the perfect career for Rosie – she is like so many girls who read celeb mags and want to be like Katie Price,' Helen said of her character. 'She is exploited by the photographer, but is not put off. She sees it as a way to make money quick without having to do much hard work.'

No one could ever accuse Katie of not working hard: in truth, she was doing more than ever. Nor had she been neglecting her great passion: horses. Katie and Alex were seen together at London's Olympia for the International Horse Show with Harvey in tow, while they sorted out what the future would hold.

Given the fact that the triangle between Katie, Pete and Alex was now becoming a national obsession, to say nothing of a massive televisual draw (Katie's appearance on *I'm A Celebrity...* and the subsequent collapse in viewing figures after she'd walked out were proof enough), every reality TV show worth its salt was trying to get in on the action and *Celebrity Big Brother* was no exception. The bosses were planning their next line-up and initially, their gaze fell on Pete. After all, given the amount of coverage her time on *I'm A Celebrity...* had generated, wouldn't this be the perfect way to take the story on? Get Pete in a house with his fellow celebs, allow the same process – claustrophobia and boredom – to break down his defences and get him to speak? This would be a huge coup and almost certain of massive ratings, too.

'Pete would be a massive scoop for *Big Brother*,' said a source on the show. 'He'd be a huge ratings winner and would certainly prove a bigger hit than Katie was in the jungle. Pete's the celebrity at the very top of the show's hit list and they've told him to name any price he wants. ITV tried to get him into the jungle and failed, so they know how big it would be to get him into the house.'

The only problem was Pete himself. Having turned down the jungle, he wasn't in the mood to spill the beans about his ex-wife: although he was happy as anyone to make his feelings known, Pete was the only one in the trio who showed occasional signs of wishing to keep schtum. Besides, he had a very packed year coming up.

'This year has been so full on, I'm looking forward to taking a week or two off,' he declared. 'This has been such a rollercoaster year. From a personal point of view it has been the worst year of my life, but professionally it has been unbelievable. I'm happier in a career point of view than ever before. The level of support I have received from people has just been incredible.'

He was still not quite ready for a new relationship, though, and was happy to say as much. Indeed, he hadn't so much as ventured out on a date. 'I just haven't felt ready, but hopefully 2010 will change all that,' he continued. 'I do get a lot of offers, though, and not just for dates. I get people sending pictures asking me to marry them. They even turn up on my door with food and cakes to ask me out, which is so sweet.'

But professionally, things really were looking up, with not only the tour but more books as well. 'I can't wait for next year,' he continued. 'I'm absolutely thrilled with the response to my tour. It's incredible to think the dates have sold out and more dates have had to be added due to the demand.

'I really didn't know how the fans' response was going to be when I first decided to release an album, so this is like a dream come true. It's been so huge that I've been asked to do a full arena tour and also tour Australia and Europe. I've got some children's and cookery books coming out as well, so it's going to be pretty amazing.'

Behind the scenes, however, a very different story was playing out. As Pete prepared to fly out to Australia alone, Christmas was fast approaching. What was particularly upsetting him was not just the fact that he would be away from his children for several weeks, but given the state of his father Savva's health, the children might not get to see their granddad again.

'This has ruined my Christmas, which is all about family,' he told a friend. 'Nothing else matters. My dad was so looking forward to seeing the kids. He's not in the best of health, so this could be the last time they might get to cuddle him. Now that precious moment has been snatched away. I've never felt so low. I fear this will be a nightmare that will go on forever. Now I am going to have to sit down and do a lot of thinking about where I go from here.'

He was right to have such concerns: given the extreme state of hostility which existed between the warring couple and the fact that neither was inclined to compromise or back down, there didn't appear to be an end in sight to this particular war. One person present after the relevant court hearing saw Pete leaving the building: 'He looked a broken man, who had the weight of the world on his shoulders,' he said. 'His eyes were bloodshot and he looked at rock bottom.'

Katie, however, was immensely relieved at the way matters had turned out. 'She's delighted with the judge's decision,' revealed a friend. 'She didn't want the kids away from her and thought they should be with their mum at such an important family time. Relations between her and Pete are so bad she saw the courts as the only way forward. It is all so sad for everyone involved.'

Pete could have fought on, but clearly he didn't know what to do for the best: 'If he goes on his own to Sydney it means he'll be apart from the children completely,' said a friend. 'He's torn between what to do for the best. Peter has tried to keep Katie happy but she has thrown it all back in his face by fighting him so hard over this trip. As far as he is concerned, there is no going back. It's an eye for an eye and tooth for a tooth. The kids haven't seen him [Savva] since February 2008 and Peter desperately wants them to get to know his father. He thought the fact that Savva is seriously ill would swing the situation in his favour, but he was proved sadly wrong. He just wanted Katie to listen to him and try and understand his point of view here. He doesn't even want to argue any more, even though he felt he had to fight his corner.'

Where was it all going to end? None of the parties looked as if they would even consider a compromise. Just how would matters pan out next?

CHAPTER 7

BIG BROTHER IS WATCHING...

*C*elebrity *Big Brother* bosses were in the final stages of some very delicate negotiations. Having seen what a difference the presence of Katie made to *I'm A Celebrity...*, they wanted to repeat that particular piece of show-business magic, and while it was too much to hope that they could tempt her back onto the screens, the drama surrounding her had been enough to turn up some other potential candidates, too. As a consequence, they had gone after Pete and when he turned them down, they turned their attentions to Alex, where they met with rather more success.

It was a couple of days before Christmas when the news filtered out that Alex would be entering the *Big Brother* house, for which he had secured a fee £150,000.

He was going in with Katie's blessing, too. After the earlier fiasco, in which his chats to the papers had prompted their split, Alex wasn't about to do anything that he hadn't run past his other half – and anyway, who better than Katie to advise him on how to handle all the attention that was bound to come his way?

'She has been giving him tips on how to handle the media and what to say when he goes on *Celeb Big Brother*,' said a friend. 'Obviously Katie doesn't want him revealing intimate secrets about herself or their relationship. She's told him to be careful about what he says and not let *CBB* bosses ply him with drink in the hope that he starts spouting off. Alex has promised her he won't be getting hammered on the show and that he won't discuss Katie's divorce from Peter Andre. Certain subjects are off limits, and that's one of them.'

Katie also viewed the opportunity in another way, too: it was an appearance on a television reality show – *I'm A Celebrity...* the first time around – that had totally transformed her image with the public and she saw the chance for Alex to achieve something similar. His own image, that of a cross-dressing cage fighter, was not one that went down entirely well with some sections of the public and here was a chance to prove that he was not a seedy character, but a man worthy of being on Katie's arm: 'Katie is really supportive of Alex and his career,' continued the friend. 'She knows she has given Alex a platform, but she isn't resentful. Alex is articulate and wants Britain to see just why she fell for him. He is a genuinely good guy.'

And so the circus moved on. Katie was never out of the limelight, at one stage even becoming the subject of some bizarre criticism from Kate Moss for wearing too much perfume. 'Have you seen Katie Price's programme?' the supermodel asked *Company* magazine. 'She wears too much. I've never actually smelt it, but she goes like this [makes enthusiastic spraying motion around head] for 10 minutes!

'I'm like, oh my God, what *is* she doing? It should be subtle enough to smell but not overdone.'

Katie was also on the receiving end of attention from Camilla Dallerup. She had clearly been keen to set the record straight about why she left, and how she and Katie had got on, and although she had spoken about this before, rumours continued to circle that the real reason she left was that Katie had arrived. According to Camilla, nothing could be further from the truth and she talked, again, about the fact that it was the production's doctors who had advised her to go.

'I've never quit anything in my life, but I was at the stage where I'd nearly passed out several times,' she said. 'Before I flew to Australia my doctor in London was really concerned about my weight because I couldn't afford to lose any more. As a dancer I'm very lean, so I had no reserves to keep me going in the jungle. I wasn't getting enough salt and sugar, and I started to get palpitations. I had memory loss, my speech was slurred and my hands were cramping – it was scary. I had to lie down after going ten steps to the toilet. Doctors were the ones to get me out, I didn't want to leave. Off-screen, the show's doctor had given me glucose tablets but they weren't enough. My doctor from London called and told me I was risking my health and should leave.'

As for Katie herself, Camilla was keen to emphasise that they couldn't have got on better, had they tried. 'There was this headline: KATIE DRIVES CAMILLA OUT OF THE JUNGLE, which was ridiculous,' she said. 'Katie could see I was in a bad way and actually told me to wake her up, if I needed to. She was so jet-lagged, but told me not to worry because she has young children and is used to getting up in the night.

'She even said I could "top and tail" with her, but we ended up sleeping in our own beds. Katie and Lucy Benjamin took it in turns – one went to bed while one looked after me.'

Camilla says she saw a more vulnerable side to Katie, which the public didn't know: 'She was really sweet and I saw a softer side to her. She was obviously still very cut up about her relationship ending, but was trying to put a brave face on it. I know what that's like because I had to work on *Strictly* after I split up with Brendan and it was awful.' So it was official – the two were the best of mates.

Meanwhile, the Katie versus Pete war continued. Pete was pictured out ice-skating with the children and Christmas Day passed with bad-tempered mutterings from all sides. The children spent some time with Pete, in the course of which his brother Michael gave Princess Tiaamii's blonde hair a little trim, provoking yet another outburst from Katie. She had become an enthusiastic Twitterer recently, and that is where she made her feelings known: '*Can't believe that when I got kids back princess comes back with her hair all cut short soo out of order,*' she tweeted, before adding, '*Pete's brother has cut princesses hair off can't put it in a pony tail why would they do that to prove what point.*'

Like so much swirling around Katie and Pete, the depths of the bad feeling between them meant that this rather trivial row got totally out of hand. 'Michael is a trained hairdresser,' said Pete's agent, Claire Powell. 'He simply trimmed Princess's hair, no more than that.'

A source close to Pete had his say: 'If Peter wanted to prove a point, he could moan about Katie sending Junior home with a bleached blond Mohican the other week. It looked awful, but Peter is not interested in point-scoring. These things should remain private, not be posted up on Twitter.'

All in all, as far as Katie was concerned, it was a

rotten end to a rotten year. Just twelve months previously, she and Pete had been married with three children: now she was a single mother involved in a very public and extremely bitter spat with a man many believe she still loved. Their break-up had come out of the blue, as far as she was concerned, and although she was clearly becoming attached to Alex, this was still a very difficult time. Katie admitted as much via another Twitter posting: '*My only wish for xmas is that my children enjoy the break along with my family,*' she said. '*I can't wait to see the back of this last year. It hasn't been the best for me personally, but these things test you and challenge you.*

'*It started all so well with many positives to look forward to as a family but it didn't quite work out like that did it?*'

But a New Year lay ahead, and with it the opportunity to once more move on. Katie marked the onset of 2010 by throwing a big party: it was both a New Year's Eve celebration and a way of sending Alex off into the *Big Brother* house in style. There was also a theme: 'Magical, enchanted, Disney or wow factor' and Katie planned to dress as a pumpkin, changing on the dot of midnight into Minnie Mouse: 'Katie's pumpkin costume will be the talk of the night,' said one friend. 'It is absolutely enormous and she can barely squeeze through the door unaided.'

Meanwhile, this was to be the last-ever *Celebrity Big Brother* and the producers were determined the series would go out in style. The house was to have a Dante's Inferno theme, complete with red carpets, fur rugs and diamante cushions. 'Hell lies in others,' Channel 4 commissioning editor David Williams rather ominously said. 'We wanted to make it more moody and atmospheric, and signal that it was going to be a little bit different. We pulled out all the stops and had some fun with it... it's slightly gothic.'

Executive producer Shirley Jones said that the participants could bring in as many clothes as they liked. 'Trust me, some of them are bringing in some amazing outfits,' she revealed. 'And others have gone over the top with how much stuff they are bringing in. We have had crate-loads arrive already.' There was also intensive speculation that Alex might enter the house as his cross-dressing alter ego, Roxanne.

'It would be nice to go out with a bang,' Shirley continued. 'We want them to be challenged, [to see] how they cope with loss of control. Celebrities tend to be quite controlling in terms of their image and their lives. A lot of the time the show works best when it is entertaining and funny... the more humiliating performance-based tasks.'

The other participants had now been named. They included the actor Stephen Baldwin, footballer-turned-actor Vinnie Jones, *Dynasty*'s Stephanie Beacham, Page Three girl Nicola T, ex-Hollywood vice madam Heidi Fleiss, Ronnie Wood's former girlfriend Ekaterina Ivanova, rapper and grime artist Lady Sovereign (Sov), singer Sisqo, singer/producer Basshunter (aka Jonas Erik Altberg) and, rather ominously given the circumstances, Katie's ex: singer Dane Bowers.

It was a line-up clearly designed to incite as much incident as possible and it had already caused controversy, not least because Kerry Katona failed to make it after she was unable to pass the relevant obligatory psychological tests, while Boy George was not allowed to join in because of restrictions in place following his release from prison. Clearly, the *Celebrity Big Brother* bosses were doing everything they could to make sparks fly.

Dane had, in fact, remained close to Katie in the years since they had first been an item, a decade previously. The previous summer, shortly after the split from Pete, he had been at her house in the early hours of the morning and the two still regarded each other as friends. Even so, Katie was a little worried that the two men living in close quarters in the *Celebrity Big Brother* household would be an explosive combination and she wanted Alex to come out of it with his image burnished, not tarnished. And so, in order that the two could meet under slightly more relaxed circumstances, she invited Dane to her New Year's Eve bash.

At first, it all seemed to go very well. Guests done up to the nines included Phill Turner and Gary Cockerill (dressed as Adam Ant), model Imogen Thomas as Dorothy from *The Wizard of Oz*, model and TV presenter Danielle Lloyd, and scores more, all dressed up for the fairyland theme. But as the night progressed, tensions began to be felt, with the result that finally, matters became totally out of hand. At around 5am, after everyone had spent the night drinking, Alex and Dane actually ended up in a fight about Katie – hardly a good omen for what was to happen in the house.

'There was always going to be trouble,' said one witness to the scene. 'Dane had a bad attitude from the moment he clapped eyes on Alex flexing his muscles. They managed to control their egos, but then all hell broke loose. They were both drunk on champagne and the two launched into one another, before being dragged apart by fellow guests. 'Katie told Dane, who was there with his girlfriend, to get out of the house,' one of them related. 'He had a bruise on his forehead already and Alex was winding him up, calling him "Jelly Belly."'

Another recounted: 'Dane still likes Katie and made it obvious as the night went on. The more he drank, the cockier he became and then had a go at Alex. He seemed to think he could flirt with Katie then insult her boyfriend – a professional cage fighter. It was around 5am when everyone was full of booze; it was handbags at twenty paces. An argument got out of hand and a punch was thrown. Alex held back. If he really wanted to do damage, he could have done but didn't; he just hit Dane the once.'

As details began to emerge, it became increasingly clear that Dane had not only been rude – and very foolish, given that Alex was a cage fighter – but an absolute pest. 'I just went,' Alex told friends afterwards. 'I put him down. He's lucky he's not dead – I'd had a few drinks, I'm trying to play it down. I never get in fights, ever. I was like, "Come on, please, let's go," and he was lairing it up. He took my kindness as a weakness.'

There were, in fact, reports that Dane had got a make-up artist to conceal the bruising so he didn't have to appear in public looking even worse. The common consensus was that he'd been a fool. 'Dane just got drunker and drunker, and thought he could abuse Alex,' a friend of Alex's reported.

Finally, Alex was prevailed on to give his version of events: in truth, it was a wonder he hadn't snapped long before. 'Me and Katie had gone to bed,' he related. 'We're in the bedroom and he's banging on the door. Anyway, basically, I let the first time go, but on the third time I got the hump and said, "What the fuck's going on?" We're there naked and I said, "What the fuck's going on?" He said, "I'm trying to get out." I spun to the door at that and he could see I was angry and thought, Oh bollocks! Then he went downstairs and I saw him rowing with somebody else. I put my clothes on and went down to try and calm it down. There were kids in the house and they were all screaming and shouting, and I was calming everyone down – I was like the peacemaker. I said, "Come on, let's not have this, let's go outside."

'I pushed him out, non-aggressively, just to get him out. I said, "Why?" and talked to him calmly. I said, "Look, I'm not shouting at you – you're getting all lairy and I'm talking to you calmly." I said, "Why did you bang on our door?" and he said, "I didn't do it." I said, "You did because I opened the door and you were banging on it." He said, "It wasn't me." I said, "All right, fair enough, you know what? I'll let that one go." Then he started lairing up with somebody else and I told him to fuck off. I said, "Look, please just go," and he said something about threatening to kill me. I just went – I'd had enough this time. I put him down, but not with a clenched hand. What put him down was a head-kick. The thing is that there were witnesses and things; there were loads of people round and it looks like I started on him, that's the silly thing. All Katie's people were here. She said to me, "It's Dane Bowers. What have you done? He's only a little weakling!" I said, "Yeah totally, but if you poke a dog with a stick enough it's going to bite." He provoked me. I had him with my other hand and kept elbowing him. He's lucky he's not dead. I'd had a few drinks.'

Nor was Alex the only person that night to lash out at Dane. 'He mounted him and hit him as well,' said Alex. 'He was the one I pulled off and told to stop fighting.'

Katie witnessed it all: 'He's full of bruises,' she said of her ex. 'He's upset and angry. He's got a massive graze on his shoulder and a massive knee.'

The timing was not brilliant, especially given the next professional engagement. Despite everything, both men decided that they would still enter the *Big Brother* house. Channel 4 was a little concerned, not least because the last thing they wanted was an onscreen fight – sparks were one thing, fisticuffs quite another – but equally they wanted the publicity the two of them would provide.

'It's a conundrum for Channel 4,' revealed a source. 'There's no doubt that some viewers will tune in hoping that Bowers and Reid will have a fight on television for them. It was always going to be prickly between them, living in the same house, but this fight ramps up the tension, but Channel 4 are also petrified of the possible consequences if things get out of hand. There was a fight on the standard version of *Big Brother* a few years ago and they were on the verge of pulling the programme off air. It would be a total disaster for them to have to pull

Celebrity Big Brother halfway through, especially because it's the last one they're doing.'

In the event, after Channel 4's head of programming held a series of top-level meetings, both Alex and Dane gave assurances that they would behave themselves once inside.

'The producers spoke to Reid and Bowers,' said a source. 'They were asked to give a full explanation of what happened on New Year's Eve and both gave their version. They both made it clear that it was a one-off dispute sparked by alcohol and that they would not cause trouble on the show. The Channel 4 team had a meeting and decided to let them stay in the show.'

And they were as good as their word. The *Celebrity Big Brother* doors opened: Dane and Alex arrived as the crowd chanted, 'Fight, fight, fight!' They declined to do so, hugging each other instead, while Alex claimed not to have had the faintest idea what had gone on at the party – clearly, it was now being pushed firmly into the past. Dane, meanwhile (who visibly had a black eye, albeit one covered in make-up), was also keen to play things down: 'I'm sorry to disappoint you, but we actually get on OK,' he told the show's host, Davina McCall. 'So what you read isn't true, interesting as it sounds.'

Katie herself, no slouch when it came to judging how people's actions came across to the public was livid and determined it wouldn't happen again. 'Katie is furious that the two of them fought at her party and the last thing she wants is for them to brawl on TV,' said a source. 'She says it makes Alex look like a thug and she wants him to come across as a gentleman and in control of his emotions. He's a kind guy, but that night Dane pushed him too far and he just snapped. Alex apologised because Katie asked him to, he loves her and doesn't want to jeopardise their relationship.'

The show kicked off well, with over 6 million viewers, and Vinnie Jones, who was being paid £350,000, was favourite to win at 5-2. 'Vinnie looks like the perfect *Big Brother* star,' said a Ladbrokes spokesman. 'He's got attitude, personality and is likely to shake the house to its foundations.'

The show kicked off with the housemates instructed to fit as many of them as possible into a Mini: all eleven managed it, although they almost failed when Lady Sovereign, Sisqo and Dane tried to sit in the boot, which was actually outside the car. Even the car had been done up to fit in with the house's faintly menacing theme: it was scarlet and black, with teeth on the fender; it was also a tight squeeze.

Meanwhile, they were all getting used to the house's new look. The Diary Room now featured a fairground theme, with a chair modelled on a waltzer ride. Fake fur pelts were scattered everywhere, along with antique animal skulls. The kitchen, designed to look like an 'autopsy room', was painted green and had stainless-steel fittings and autopsy jars: it was all a little unnerving, as it was meant to be. There were communal bedrooms, with Big Brother handing out earplugs to protect any celebrities who were disturbed by anyone else's snores.

Unsurprisingly, Alex's penchant for cross-dressing was an early subject for the house. Stephanie told him that he was a 'cross-dressing bad boy', which had him laughing: 'I dress up for fun, they've just blown it way out of proportion,' he said. Indeed, he admitted, this had partly been what had helped him to attract Katie: 'If it's going to get me a hot woman, which it did, I'll dress up whatever.'

Stephen, meanwhile, was curious to know whether Alex had brought a man's or a woman's wardrobe: 'All Arthur, no Martha,' said Alex, before pouring cold water on reports that he'd been offered an extra £100,000 for wearing women's clothing – 'I'd wear a dress for 100 grand,' he said.

Alex appeared to be rather keen to impress Vinnie, and began by asking him about his training regime. 'It used to be half ten to half one, Monday to Friday,' Vinnie replied. 'And then you would go and do weights, and that two or three times a week.' And as for when he was in *X-Men 3*: 'That was three months in the gym!' was his reply.

But matters cooled somewhat when Alex told Heidi,

'He [Vinnie] used to be a bad boy, not so much any more, but he has still got a bit of the image.'

'We all get older – it will happen to you, mate, don't worry,' Vinnie snapped and the conversation never really recovered after that.

Katie was watching it all while she hosted a dinner party at her mansion: 'When Dane appeared, she booed and said Alex would wipe the floor with him in there,' a friend said.

But as events began to unfold inside the house, there were stirrings of trouble on the outside as well. The full ramifications of what happened at the New Year's Eve party continued to work their way through, with further allegations that Dane was also angry that the children were up so late, allegedly shouting, 'Why are you letting the kids be up well past midnight?' And then, to make matters worse, although the guests had signed confidentiality agreements (the party was to feature on Katie's reality TV show), some posted pictures on Facebook, which illustrated quite clearly that the children had been up and about throughout much of the night. Pete, still angry that he had not been allowed to take the children to Australia, was livid and made this clear, too.

'The children are Pete's top priority,' said a friend. 'He's not happy about what's happened and will do everything he can to protect them. Peter is absolutely furious: he can't believe anybody would go off like that with kids in the house. Little children should not be exposed to this and they shouldn't even have been there. They should have been enjoying themselves in Australia with their dad. Peter's heartbroken they aren't with him in Australia; it is hard enough for him missing them without having to hear about the violence. What sort of a mum stops her children from going on holiday with their dad and then keeps them at a party? It's not the sort of place little ones should be.'

It was clear that hostilities were as bitter as ever. Not one to take accusations lying down, Katie came back with a retort of her own: 'It was a family party and there were lots of children there with nannies to look after them,' said a friend. 'Princess and Junior enjoyed themselves and were in bed long before the fight, so knew nothing about it.'

It was all rather unfortunate and the various parties who had been around when it happened were trying to play it down. Alex, of course, was on view twenty-four hours a day, still not getting on entirely well with Vinnie, but chatting away happily enough to the other housemates. He mentioned the injuries he had sustained through infighting and Stephen suggested he have surgery to sort out the problem, if he should decide to embark on a Hollywood career.

Stephen, a member of the famous Baldwin acting clan,

was enjoying himself in the house, too. The very glamorous Stephanie Beacham provided a diversion and he was able to chat to her about his past drug addiction: 'I just deal with it one day at a time,' he said. 'When you have a complicated mind – and most of us do, because we're a complicated species – it's just getting around the simple thought of "just not today". It's such a simple thought. When you can just get through twenty-four hours, you can start over again.'

Stephanie's sympathetic response produced a well of emotion from him, too: 'I think I have a bit of a platonic crush on Stephanie,' he confided. 'It's shocking. I think she's just delightful. It's just a nice, friendly, healthy little infatuation.' Stephanie was providing a fair bit of entertainment herself, brushing her teeth while wearing sunglasses and complaining about the facilities. 'I'm surprised the loo doesn't shut and the showers are so small, but it's jolly and sweet in the house,' she said.

Although the producers of the show were clearly hoping that Alex would be its biggest draw (and in some ways they would be proved right), it was Ekaterina, known as Katia, who was attracting a fair bit of attention from the outset. A couple of the younger men in the household seemed rather taken with her, starting with Sisqo: 'Kat – I don't know, I could be wrong,' he said. 'I'm a little interested. It seems like she's got a lot of layers. When she first came into the house, she seemed maybe a little shy at first, and then, you know, when we were out there in the smoking area, she seemed to open up a little bit more. I'm kind of curious.' But he had competition from Basshunter, who had told Davina on entering the house: 'I'm going to touch base and then I'm going to do some hunting.' Could he be hunting Katia? He, too, headed outside for a cigarette with her, gallantly offering her his coat as he did so. There was nothing reality TV producers liked more than a little on-screen romance – *à propos* Katie and Pete – and there were high hopes that something more would develop here.

But the attention was never going to be away from Alex for long. The nation was just too interested in the ongoing saga with him, Katie and Pete to let it rest and matters were inadvertently helped along by Vinnie, who it appeared, had not been following as closely as everyone else. It had to be explained to him that Alex and Dane shared the same ex: 'I just got filled in on everything,' he said. 'When did Dane get involved with Jordan?'

'Eight, nine years ago,' said Dane.

'Oh, before Peter?' asked Vinnie. 'I like Peter.'

Alex unwisely joined in. 'You pals with him, are you?' he asked Vinnie. 'Come on then, let's go.' But he then calmed down, adding, 'I'm cool with him [Pete], I'm actually cool with him. All this Team Andre, Team Pricey, it's just the media.'

'But it's only fun [to read about] if it's bad,' Heidi pointed out.

Alex replied that it was stressful for those involved.

'You've got to be big enough to handle that,' said Heidi.

Vinnie pointedly asked Alex whether he had actually met Pete: Alex had to admit the answer was no.

This exchange appeared to increase Vinnie's irritation with everything to do with the show. In the Diary Room, he seemed to be complaining about Alex, although he didn't mention him by name, saying, 'Tabloid celebrities – I think some of them are here. I don't really know any of them and some are trying a bit hard in here.' He also hinted that he might leave early: cabin fever appeared to be taking its toll. 'I don't fancy doing three weeks. I keep eyeing those walls to see how high they are.' Later Dane asked him what he would like for his forty-fifth birthday, which happened to be that very day: 'A red card straight from here would do me,' was his reply.

So, was Alex allowed to talk about Katie or wasn't he? There had been many reports in the press to the effect that Katie had forbidden him from doing any such thing, but Alex didn't appear to be heeding the warning. 'I think I've met the person that I want to spend the foreseeable future with,' he told Nicola T. The nation held its breath.

Nor was Katie exactly making any attempt to quell

the level of public interest in what was going on. A rumour had surfaced that the former TV presenter Vikki Thomas might be sent into the house: she had quite a lot in common with Katie, given that not only was she a past glamour model, but she had also slept with both Alex and Dane. Katie commented on these matters of state as she always did, namely on Twitter: '*Heard a model called Vikki Thomas, who is an ex of Dane's and Alex's, is going into the house. How funny, love it,*' she tweeted. Vikki did nothing to stop the speculation: 'Watch this space,' she wrote. Alas, it was not to be: Channel 4 denied any such plans were afoot.

Meanwhile, the housemates got on with their tasks. Vinnie was called into a telephone box in the garden, while the others were set chores to try and free him: these included Stephen Baldwin getting his hands caught in mousetraps and Dane carrying manure around. Then Stephanie, Vinnie and Sov had to put an item of food on their head while the others fired paintballs at it in an attempt to win it: they managed to get their hands on milk, cheese, mayonnaise, ketchup and fajitas. Alex encouraged Nicola to fire her paintball at Vinnie's privates, she duly obliged and so the fun went on.

But outside the house, speculation continued to mount. Just how was Katie reacting to everything that was going on inside? Would she and Alex be an item when he came out? Just what, really, did the future hold?

CHAPTER 8

ALEX V VINNIE

They had been in the house a couple of days now and there was no doubting it: Alex and Vinnie simply weren't getting along. Perhaps the reason was that they were too similar: both were self-made hard men with a background in sports. Or maybe it was because they were too different: Vinnie was a footballer-turned-Hollywood actor, if not quite A-list status, then at least a very big celebrity, whereas Alex's fame was entirely due to the fact that he'd appeared in the papers a lot with Katie.

Indeed, it was his open boasting about that which irritated Vinnie still more. The two of them constantly sparred verbally, with Vinnie seemingly using every occasion to needle Alex – and Alex walking only too willingly into the trap. In the longer term, this was to act very much in his favour: Katie had wanted the world to see that underneath the muscles, the dresses and the bravado, Alex was actually a genuinely nice man, and so it was to turn out. But he was, as some of the other housemates were beginning to realise, in many ways rather naive. He simply didn't understand the way he sometimes came across and he certainly didn't realise that he quite frequently made himself look like an idiot. One early example was comparing the fuss surrounding the soap opera he had found himself caught up in with the uproar over the sudden and unexpected death of one of the greatest entertainers of the age.

'In the summer in the press, the two big stories were Michael Jackson dying and Kate and Peter splitting, and me,' said Alex, as they all relaxed in the house. 'People don't like Kate and it's Saint Peter. I don't think I am good for Kate's image because of the custody battle that's going on. I've had to grow up a lot over the last six months. It's been a steep learning curve for me.'

He was certainly being pretty open about the fact that his image was not, perhaps, all it could be, but the Michael Jackson comparison had Vinnie snapping at him once more. 'Why don't you all just sit around a table and discuss it like grown-ups?' Vinnie asked.

'I'd love to,' Alex replied, before turning to the subject of the children and the effect it was having on them.

'You know, those kids are going to grow up and see all this and they don't want to grow up and see nasty things about their mum,' he went on. As for whether he was planning on having his own family – that was his next big adventure, he told Stephanie, and although the public was pretty curious as to Katie's views on the subject, on this one at least, she was keeping schtum.

Everyone was pretty fascinated by what was going on inside the house, but nothing would ever detract attention from Katie for any length of time outside, and so it proved again. Whatever she did, she continued to make headlines and now it was her beauty care regime that was put up for inspection – and it was a long way from being what the doctor recommended. She had a new book out about how to look good, *Standing Out*, and she was perfectly happy to dole out advice herself.

'Looking after my skin is not my strong point, but the two things that do make my skin look better are sun beds and Botox,' she revealed. 'I used to use spray tan, but it stinks, so now I use sun beds. I know people say they're dangerous and can give you skin cancer but I don't smoke, I hardly drink and we've all got to die of something, so that's just my choice. I get my forehead and around my eyes Botoxed every six months and I love it. You can't beat it.'

In fact, this was not a regime that would do her any

favours in the long term. Not only did sun-bed usage increase the risk of skin cancer, as she'd said, but it also damaged the skin. Katie kept herself very deeply tanned and Botox or not (which many would argue she was still much too young to need), this would make her extremely wrinkly in the longer term.

As for make-up, Katie's enthusiasm was undisguised, although at least in this case she wasn't acting against established medical advice: 'I don't wear any make-up if I'm not working, but if I'm doing a shoot, going out or appearing on TV, I'm like a drag queen,' she said. 'I like lots and lots of products; in fact, I like the whole of the Boots counter. I wear Dior Showgirl mascara, lipstick by Bourjois, Mac or Stila, and Mac eyeliner and eye shadow. I'm also a big fan of false lashes and I love Mac again.' All of this was an understatement, but Katie knew as well as anyone how to attract attention – she'd had years of practice – and it was the secret of a memorable look.

But not everyone appreciated it. A lot of the work that Katie was having done, such as Botox, was actually meant for more mature women and some people felt she was pushing it too far. She also appeared to be using fillers, again more suitable for much older women, and her face by now bore little resemblance to the fresh-faced ingénue she'd been a decade earlier. Around this time a survey had appeared in the press citing men saying that they preferred women who didn't use too much make-up: Katie was mentioned widely as being a prime example of people who took it too far.

The actress Amanda Donohoe, who was about fifteen years older than Katie, certainly felt that the Pricey was being a little unwise. 'Younger women who don't need anything doing are having procedures because they're feeling insecure,' she said. 'It's so, so sad and it's about people taking your money and running. Once you start it, where do you finish?

'You see someone like Katie Price and think, what are you going to look like when you're 50? She looks like some kind of generic doll. I thought she looked beautiful as she was. Young women look at that as an ideal, but it isn't – it isn't even normal.'

But it certainly got her noticed. Even that renowned man of letters, Martin Amis, acknowledged as much, although his phrasing was scarcely complimentary: 'All we are really worshipping is two bags of silicone,' he said. He was also totally wrong: there were plenty of other glamour girls out there who'd had their assets enhanced to get in the papers, but none of them had struck a chord with the public like Katie had. The public warmed to her for, say what you like about the girl, she was a fighter. She had been very publicly dumped and this was by no means the first of her man troubles: Katie had had rotten luck with men throughout her life and when she became pregnant with Harvey, her son by Dwight Yorke, she found herself a single mother to boot. She also clearly doted on her children, however much she might have been criticised for letting them stay up late: the woman was far more than just another model going along for the ride.

Back in the *Big Brother* house, events were moving along nicely. It had been hinted at for some time that a mystery guest would soon appear and so it proved, although this was not an ex of Alex and Dane's, rather the international socialite, Ivana Trump. She was introduced in a very stylish manner: Sisqo had been performing magic tricks, using Lady Sovereign as his glamorous assistant; he made her disappear, but when he went to reintroduce her, it turned out to be not the Lady, but la Trump waiting in the wings.

If the series' makers wanted to go out with a bang, they were certainly succeeding. While some of the housemates' identities might have taxed a few members of the general public, there were some genuine stars in there. Most notable, of course, had been Vinnie and Stephanie, but Ivana was an inspired choice. The ex-wife of the US property mogul Donald Trump, who was in the throes of divorcing her fourth husband, Rossano Rubicondi, twenty-four years her junior (and a reality TV participant in his own right), Ivana was stylish, sophisticated and used to making an impact wherever she went. This was a triumph for the organisers, who were clearly thrilled with their prize.

It was to prove quite an experience for all the contestants. Ivana herself, rather like Stephanie, was certainly slumming it compared to her usual lifestyle, but she knew what she was doing. No one in the world was as aware of the impact of media appearances as Ivana Trump, not even Katie Price – after all, Ivana had been doing it for thirty years before Katie arrived on the scene – and she knew that constant onscreen exposure would benefit her in some way, even if she wasn't entirely sure what that benefit might be.

'I'm expecting... I'm a businesswoman, a marketing woman. I will be meeting people I totally don't know,' Ivana told Davina before she went in. 'It will be a totally new experience and from that will come a book; I'm a little bit of the high maintenance.' She certainly was that: for a short time, it even seemed as Ivana Trump would deflect attention from Alex and his love triangle – although ultimately, even she couldn't manage that.

It was unclear what Stephanie made of it all: before Ivana appeared, she had commented, 'I think someone really truly troublesome will come in next. I'm sure I could be expected to be more troublesome than I am.' It was not clear how the arrangements were going to pan out, either, because although there were twelve dining chairs for the now full compliment of twelve celebrities, there were only eleven beds. When putting together a series such as this, the producers use all sorts of psychological tricks to stir up as much tension as they can and this was clearly one of them.

Meanwhile, the fun and games continued. Someone in the production team had a sense of humour: they got Dane to dress up as Kylie Minogue to Alex's Jason Donovan for a duet: 'Especially For You', the song made famous by Kylie and Jason when they really were an item, back in 1988. Both Dane and Alex had to wear wigs: Dane's was a curly blond one, while Alex's was straight blond. Although Dane looked a little uncomfortable as they sang, the two took it in good part. There was some surprise in certain quarters that it was Dane who had to dress as a woman for the task, not Alex, but someone, somewhere, had enjoyed working it all out.

Vinnie, meanwhile, was a ventriloquist, with Stephen as his doll – Stephen had to sit on his knee and parrot words; Heidi, Jonas, Nicola T and Katia were instructed to perform the Can-Can. While it would be pushing it to say that everyone had become best friends by now and there was still some understated tension between Vinnie and Alex, there had been no heated displays of temper. Everyone was getting on just fine.

Indeed, in some ways the producers could have been forgiven for wishing for more of a spark because it made for such good television. However, in the wake of events in the recent past, everyone felt that caution still had to be the key. Three years earlier, a row had blown up into a near international incident over the perceived bullying of the Indian actress Shilpa Shetty by a band of her fellow housemates, led, sadly, by the late Jade Goody. The two had kissed and made up very publicly after that, but Channel 4 was aware that it had to proceed with great caution: sparks were good, but genuine fury was not. They had had to emphasise as much to Dane and Alex before they went into the house and had no reason to change their point of view.

Amid reports that Katie had bet Alex £20,000 that he wouldn't win *Celebrity Big Brother* (she was to be called on to pay out, if he did), it began to look as if Heidi might be first to leave. She was homesick, she said, and missed her parrots (she kept them back home in Nevada), her shower and food. The other contestants tried to persuade her to stay put.

'You're not doing it, Heidi Fleiss,' said Nicola. 'You can't do it. You know what, it must be so much worse for you. I've got a bit of a safety net because I know that the minute I walk out, within an hour I can probably be with Poppy [her baby daughter].'

'I definitely want to come say hey to the parrots at some point,' added Lady Sovereign, but this just appeared to make matters worse.

'I have to see them tomorrow, I can't do it any more,' said Heidi, who also admitted that she had personal issues to confront – her brother had very tragically drowned shortly before she went into the house.

'Can we give you a facial or something pathetic like that?' asked Stephanie.

Heidi said that was sweet, but that she was already 'in the zone'.

The housemates were clearly forming a bond. Stephanie told Vinnie that she was 'surprisingly upset' by Heidi's desire to go. Heidi, though, was very obviously down. 'I'm not comfortable any more,' she told the Diary Room. 'I don't like the shower, I want my food; I want my things.'

Heidi had been a surprise choice for the house. She had become famous when she kept a brothel supplying ladies of the night to some of Hollywood's biggest stars (only Charlie Sheen had been named, but it was known there were many, many more) and she had finally ended up in prison, although this was more for tax evasion than anything else. In the wake of the conviction, she had given up her old job and moved to a ranch in Nevada, where she ended up opening a laundrette. She was not so much famous as extremely notorious, and although an odd choice for the show, she made the line-up an interesting mix. Just as everyone hoped Alex would spill the beans about Katie, so they also hoped that Heidi would spill the beans about her ex-clientèle but, as she told Davina on entering the house: 'That isn't my style.'

Ivana, however, was settling in well. She was an old trooper and there was no chance whatsoever that she would have gone in at all, had she feared that she might not be able to cope. Indeed, she couldn't have been happier. 'So far everyone is fantastic,' she told the Diary Room. 'It is going to be humbling experience and definitely one of the hardest challenges and you never know, I might write a book about it.' And she had certainly put her experiences down in book form in the past: in the wake of her divorce, it was Ivana who coined the phrase: 'Don't get mad – get everything'. She had turned this into several self-help books and novels, and showed every sign of thinking that her current set-up might present an opportunity to do so again.

So, what did people think of her? 'I think people think I'm a hard worker, which I am,' Ivana replied. 'They think I'm a good businesswoman, which I am. Women look at me as a role model, which I know.' Not everyone was so gracious: Stephen was expressing fears that Ivana might be a 'sleep cougar' and expressed a desire to sleep further away from her. A 'cougar' was the new term for older women who dated younger men: Stephen appeared to think that semi-conscious, older women could be even more of a threat.

Meanwhile, the Vinnie and Alex show continued. The animosity appeared to have gone, although Vinnie was certainly adept at winding his adversary up. Alex admitted that he had bet on himself in the past: 'Why?' asked Vinnie. 'You've had two wins and nine losses, haven't you?'

He then demanded to know why Alex was so open about the cross-dressing. 'I'm ex-army – we all dress up for a laugh,' said Alex.

'Do you sit at home in a dress?' demanded Vinnie.

'I have done,' said Alex. 'Not by myself. I sat at home with a dress on with a friend of mine. To see what it's all about. Some people wear nappies...'

'Some people keep that to themselves,' Vinnie responded. 'They don't let newspapers know about it.'

Alex went off to do a workout: 'I ask him on purpose,' Vinnie told Heidi and Dane. 'He seems to like it, he seems a bit too honest for his own good sometimes.' That was almost certainly the case. Vinnie in some ways exuded an almost protective aura when talking about Alex now: he himself had been in the public eye for many years and knew far more about the pitfalls than Alex. Sometimes it almost seemed as if he wanted to warn the younger man.

The drama outside the house continued, with various revelations coming out about its inmates, but this time, surprisingly enough, the latest one involved

Stephanie Beacham. Her thirty-five-year-old daughter Phoebe, in a confession she later came to regret, revealed that Stephanie's £100,000 fee for taking part in the show would actually be spent on helping Phoebe deal with her addiction to cocaine. 'I owe her everything,' Phoebe said. 'My mother saved my life. If it wasn't for her, I wouldn't be here today. I owe her so much. I was a total wild child, but Mum has always been there. She has spent literally thousands of pounds of her hard-earned money getting me out of all kinds of scrapes.'

Phoebe went on to reveal that she had started smoking dope at the age of eighteen before moving on to cocaine, that the previous year she had drunk something spiked with Ketamine at the Glastonbury Festival, after which she had slashed her wrists, and that following counselling sessions, she had been diagnosed with bipolar disorder. 'I've been totally clean for a year now and the doctors have discovered the right medication. It has totally changed my life, I feel so well.'

Stephanie, though, was not best pleased when she discovered the story had come out. Apart from anything else, Phoebe had a child and Stephanie clearly felt this should have been kept away from the public domain.

No matter. Back inside the house, tensions between Vinnie and Alex had visibly lifted even more: 'I thought

Alex was a first-class prat when he first came in,' Vinnie, who appeared to have abandoned all thoughts of leaving early himself, told Stephanie. 'And now I've gone, "Hold on, he's not a bad lad at all."'

Stephanie thought so too. Alex was, 'incredibly, delightfully naive,' she said.

'He's only been in the public eye for six months. I done the same – you say silly things and it sticks,' said Vinnie, who was by now sounding dangerously close to being sympathetic. 'The cross-dressing, he's no more a cross-dresser than I am! You say things early on and it sticks with you for twenty, thirty years.' Could an unlikely friendship be developing in there? Stranger things have happened.

Alex was then called upon to put on a display that really could cause tensions with the others, had they not guessed that he was only obeying orders. Jonas had built a big snowman in the area outside the *Big Brother* house, where it stood in all its icy grandeur – but not for long. Alex was told by the Tree of Temptation (a tree in the garden which would speak to housemates and try to cause mischief) to, 'kick the shit out of the snowman,' in a display of Mixed Martial Arts skills: the snowman was dressed in a khaki headband for the session, and so Alex set about demolishing it with a few well-aimed kicks. He leapt up in the air, used his feet to take it out and soon all that was left was a much smaller mound of snow that formed the base – all the careful workmanship was no more.

At first his fellow celebs looked horrified, but they soon realised that he was doing it for a reason and applauded him when he told them that he had to, 'get some aggression out.' His reward for this was an hour with a real punchbag, something else he couldn't tell the others about – but everyone ended up friends. But this, too, was an example of the psychological testing that the contestants were being put through: to have to engage in bizarre behaviour without telling anyone the reason why could very easily have caused mayhem. But it didn't. Even Jonas seemed to understand nothing personal was going on and similarly to his snowman, he took it like a man.

Everyone else was calming down, too. Heidi Fleiss had cheered up and decided to stay after all: 'I have no idea what was making me so irritable,' she admitted. Jonas/Basshunter and Katia were getting positively frolicsome, kissing and cuddling in front of the others, although Katia warned him that she always ended up in relationships: she had not been single since the age of fourteen, she said. What her ex Ronnie Wood made of it all was unclear: he was keeping his own counsel and probably very wisely, too.

Jonas certainly appeared to be completely smitten with the young Russian. 'She's so funny, always smiling,' he told the Diary Room. 'You don't meet that kind of people often. Especially being very pretty and cute as well, that's a bonus. I feel there's a connection between us, but I think she feels really bad that she's got a boyfriend. I like her – I like her very much. Sometimes you have to be a little bit selfish, I think. I'm very, very happy that I met Kat. I hope she feels the same way.'

All the while there was intense speculation as to how far the couple's ardour would progress onscreen – unlike some other countries, Britain had yet to experience a live *Big Brother* bonk – with one of Jonas's exes confidently predicting the couple would go the whole hog. As it turned out, she was wrong.

Back outside, not for the first time, Katie was blowing hot and cold. She had never liked the implication that anyone, above all her menfolk, were making themselves famous on the back of what she'd achieved, and it was beginning to look as if she thought Alex was going too far. 'He's living off my fame in there,' she is reputed to have snapped to a friend. 'He's only famous because he's with me, anyway. He's doing the exact opposite of what I told him to do! I can't believe it.'

This should have come as no surprise. There had been a similar temper tantrums just a few weeks earlier, after she left the jungle, and one ongoing cause of contention with Pete had been the full extent of the other's fame. Katie had always felt – and made it clear not only to

Pete, but to everyone else, too – that it was she who had rescued him from a life of obscurity: his pop career had been over for years by the time they'd met and it was only in the wake of their relationship that it perked up once more. Who knows how influential she had really been in all this? Pop careers wax and wane, and there was every chance that Pete would have made it big again, even if he hadn't met Katie. But together, the two undoubtedly turned out to be bigger than the sum of their parts.

And now, in Katie's eyes, it seemed to be happening all over again with Alex. A position like hers is a difficult one, of course: all famous people constantly question the motives of those that surround them, asking themselves whether they are wanted for themselves or their fame. But Katie had allowed a combination of that fear and her own competitiveness to destroy her relationship with Pete and there was a danger that she might do the same with Alex – which would be a shame because, as Vinnie and Stephanie had observed, he was turning out to be nothing like his public image. And if he cared about Katie, she would hardly be helping her own chances of happiness by pushing him away.

But Katie was never one to do things by halves, and once she got the bit between her teeth, she worried and worried it until it could scarcely be worried any more. She went further, threatening that she would not be around to greet Alex when he came out of the house. 'Jordan's gone ballistic and turned into Godzilla after seeing him this week,' revealed a friend. 'She told him clearly before he went in not to trade off her fame, but she hates what she's seeing every night.'

Alex had certainly been talking about Katie, that much was true. But given the fact that they had briefly broken up after he publicly spoke of being on the verge of proposing when she was in the celebrity jungle, it seemed very unlikely that Alex would be doing any of this deliberately. Nor had he actually revealed very much – there had been the odd comment about Pete, about his own image and the impact the furore was having on the children, but there had been no bedroom secrets revealed, and not even an insight into what really caused the break-up with Pete. Given what he could have made public, Alex was being relatively discreet. The real culprit was the surroundings in which he now found himself. Given they were totally cut off from the outside world and making their own reality, it was easy for the housemates to forget that every blink, every cough was being filmed for posterity. There was no privacy in here, none at all. Confidences that appeared to be whispered to just one person were broadcast to millions. It was the *Big Brother* house, after all.

'He went into the house knowing how volatile Katie can be, but after a couple of days there, it's as if he's forgotten he's being filmed,' said a friend. Indeed, this seemed to be the most likely explanation. Alex wanted to get more serious with Katie, not less. But was he going too far? Would his indiscretions, mild as they were, bring a halt to the new romance?

CHAPTER 9

KATIE LASHES OUT

There were now two shows pulling in an audience: Alex and the housemates in the *Celebrity Big Brother* household and Katie and her friends watching it all from outside. And it was difficult to say which one was attracting more attention. Katie was indisputably the star of both shows, for viewers were still hoping that Alex was going to be indiscreet and spill the beans – but so far, at least, they were disappointed.

The ramifications of that now notorious New Year's Eve party continued to rumble on. A post went up on YouTube with a video of the party: it showed Katie dressed up as Minnie Mouse and looking very the worse for wear, drunkenly counting down to midnight, while yelling, 'I hate 2009. I hate it, I hate it, I hate it!' In the background was the voice of a child: it could quite clearly be heard shouting, 'Don't say it, Mummy, don't!' Katie was then shown dressed in her pyjamas, singing Taylor Dayne's 'Tell It To My Heart'.

Katie was apoplectic with rage. The culprit was soon revealed to be another glamour model, Chelsea White, and she lost no time in revealing her feelings on Twitter: '*NEVER trust chelseawhite.co.uk as a friend she is disloyal can't be trusted shes a grass she will make a quick buck off anyone a parasite,*' she blasted. For a start the guests had all signed confidentiality agreements, on top of which any footage that made it into the public domain was due to be via Katie's reality show. To describe her as angry was to say that an erupting volcano was a little warm: rarely had she been seen to be so furious before.

Chelsea, however, was not slow to fight back. '*No video or story was EVER sold on my behalf to Newspapers,*' she wrote on her personal blog. '*The innocent video of me and my friend Imogen dancing at Katie's New Year's Eve Party has been taken from youtube and has been edited to a much shorter version. I cannot believe Katie Price, a woman in her 30s of 3 children has decided to start a hate campaign against me on the likes of facebook, twitter etc for something that I haven't done. Statements that Katie is making are nothing but false accusations.*' And so the rows rumbled on.

There were problems on the Pete front, too. The saga of Princess's hair had not gone away: Pete was still smarting about the fact that Katie had made her complaints public, possibly because he was also smarting about a much bigger grievance, namely that he hadn't been able to take the children to Australia. 'That was the most pathetic thing to get brought out into the public domain,' he said. 'It was a trim off the ends of her hair, for God's sake; it was so pathetic. My daughter's hair needed a trim, what's the problem? The truth is Princess had come to me a few times with hair straightened by straightening irons, which used to annoy me, so I had to get it trimmed. These things should be private, it's so childish, why would she do that?'

But everything was now a battleground between the two of them. Whether it was Princess's hair, trips to Australia, New Year's Eve parties, Alex or anything else, the atmosphere just seemed to become ever more bitter. The grievances in the marriage had been building up for a long time before they burst out, and now they had done so, there was no stopping them. If Katie had said it was sunny outside, Pete would have observed that it was raining, and vice versa. There was no common ground between them: even the children had become a bone of contention, although both insisted their interests should always come first. Katie also admitted to using straighteners on Princess's hair – that had not yet blown up into a proper row, but it was about to – saying, 'She has naturally curly blonde hair, which I straightened recently and it didn't look good – she looked like a little troll.' It was yet another spat that would shortly dominate the front pages.

Back in the *Big Brother* house, Alex continued to entertain the nation, but even that was causing Katie concern. Fiercely competitive as ever, she was still determined, just as she had been with Pete, that she should always be the one with the higher profile in whatever relationship she was in. 'Katie is obsessed with watching him on TV,' a source told *Heat* magazine. 'She keeps on saying, "He's not as famous as me, though," like it's some sort of weird mantra; she's really paranoid about it. She's not used to being the half of the couple who's out of the public eye and it's really unnerving her.'

Not that Katie was exactly out of the spotlights, but unlike Alex, she wasn't appearing on television every night. And given that Alex was doing so, she was very keen that the public thought she had made a good choice with her new man, too. 'She's been saying, "He's nice, yeah?" over and over again, as if she's trying to persuade herself,' continued the source. 'But a lot of her close mates secretly think he's playing up to the cameras and being really fake and kissing ass. They think he's been a bit of an idiot so far.' Then again, that had been Vinnie Jones's initial reaction and he'd soon changed his mind.

The other inmates continued to attract attention, but it was very much a side show compared to the story of the Katie trio. There was a lovers' tiff: Jonas told Katia she was only in the show because of her relationship with Ronnie Wood, an entirely true assertion that ended up reducing her to tears. He 'didn't know anything about her,' sniffed Katia, although the duo soon kissed and made up. Which of the housemates, Katia asked him, would he most like to be stuck on a desert island with? 'You,' Jonas replied. Alex, rather surprisingly, contributed to this debate by telling Katia that she and Jonas could be the new Katie and Pete – a status that a fair few people were under the assumption he wanted for himself.

He was certainly making his mark. The longer he stayed in the house, the more Alex appeared to relax into it: he was openly talking about Pete, now, saying that he'd like to sit down with him to clear the air and would be pleased if Pete entered the *Big Brother* house (Pete's feelings can only be imagined). Then Alex put on various displays, running around the house completely naked, just covering his privates with his hands, as well as sporting a bright pink mankini, which at least showed off his tan. Vinnie, in a matey sort of way, asked if he regretted running around naked: 'I regret that, but I'm Alex Reid – you either love me or you hate me,' he replied.

The tensions in the house now appeared to be moving towards the women. Katia had not proved popular among her fellow females and indeed, some of the men: apart from the on/off flirtation with Jonas (and Katia *did* have a boyfriend on the outside), she just didn't appear to be contributing, according to some of them at least. 'She definitely is not a likeable character,' Heidi told Vinnie. 'She never talks. She never says anything, but giggles with Sov like an idiot.'

Vinnie appeared to agree, mimicking Katia's laugh. 'They both act like idiots. Sov is always complaining and whining,' Heidi continued. 'They never have an opinion or a comment; they just sit there and giggle like idiots.'

Meanwhile, the games carried on: ten of the housemates were required to act as OAPs, while Ivana and Stephanie were their care workers, a role that appeared, much to Vinnie's disgust, to consist of liquidising all the food, while in the 'Klapped-Out Factor' obstacle course, Vinnie had to throw tea all over himself. It was all fun and games.

Whatever her private thoughts, Katie was still being extremely supportive. She took to Twitter again: '*My man Alex is doing soooo well an miss him sooo much sooo proud*,' she tweeted.

Even so, by Katie's standards, she was keeping a relatively low profile, perhaps aware that if she was out there working the public then it really would look as if

Above: Katie looks extremely relieved as she leaves the *I'm a Celebrity* camp.

© *ITV/Rex Features*

Below left: Alex at Brisbane Airport. He had reportedly flown to Australia to ask Katie to marry him, but Katie then ended their relationship live on air during her interview with presenters Ant and Dec.

© *Brian Cassey/Rex Features*

Below right: Katie arrives back at Heathrow Airport after her stint in the jungle.

© *Dennis Stone/Rex Features*

Katie looking gorgeous at the British Comedy Awards in December 2009.

© Jonathan Hordle/Rex Features

Above: Katie shares a joke with Jonathan Ross and Alan Carr at the British Comedy Awards.

© *Ken McKay/Rex Features*

Below: Katie is constantly in demand – here, she is promoting her latest book and her range of equestrian wear.

© *Geoffrey Robinson/David Hartley/Rex Features*

Above: Katie out and about with Harvey in the snow in December 2009.

Below: Alex leaving his house to head to the *Celebrity Big Brother* house and,
below right, entering the house itself.

Katie wows the crowds at the National Television Awards in January 2010, while Alex was winning fans of his own in the *Big Brother* house.

© *David Fisher/Rex Features*

Alex celebrates being crowned the winner of *Celebrity Big Brother 2010*.

Above: Alex and Katie arrive in Las Vegas for their February 2nd wedding.

Below left: The happy couple arrive back in the UK.

Below right: Katie shows off her wedding ring for the first time, as she leaves the Radio One studios after an interview with DJ Chris Moyles.

Katie's stunning diamond-encrusted wedding ring.

she and Alex were locked in a battle to see who could get the most publicity. Of course, Alex wasn't the only one inside the house to talk about Katie. Dane and Stephanie engaged in a conversation in which Katie was never actually mentioned by name, but in which she appeared to figure very largely: it began when Dane told Stephanie that men prefer to see their womenfolk without make-up.

'I think you *think* you do,' Stephanie replied.

'No, we do,' said Dane. 'Otherwise we wouldn't be with them. Don't get me wrong, I don't like everyone with no make-up on. Some people should just keep it painted on. If you find a girl you can look at with no make-up on and you prefer it, that's what it's about. I hate lots of make-up on anyone. A lot of people don't know how to do their make-up properly.' Did he have anyone in mind?

The attention moved back to Alex. Vinnie had clearly decided to offer him some paternal advice, telling him that his relationship with Katie might be having a detrimental effect on his career, and that if he really wanted to make a success of the movies, he would have to stop talking so much about his private life. 'No one is going to want to be in a movie with you,' Vinnie told him bluntly. 'If you offered me $5 million to be in a movie with you I would say no, I can't be involved. Are you worried that if you don't say you're a cross-dresser and a gay, then you won't be on the front page of the newspaper? If you don't want to be on the front pages for that, then stop saying it! If you are a cross-dresser, you don't admit it.' But making the front pages was becoming as important to Alex as it was to Katie – after all, it had changed his life.

But Vinnie seemed keen to make a point here: he brought up the increasingly embarrassing episode in which Alex had been on the brink of proposing to Katie live on television, only for her to dump him.

'Like I'd propose on national TV, that's such a load of bullshit,' Alex replied.

'I read it on the Internet,' said Vinnie.

'Did you actually split up?' piped up Dane.

'She binned you on national TV in front of 12 million viewers,' Vinnie continued.

Alex looked sombre: 'I wasn't going to talk about that, but since you asked,' he began. 'I got texts from her saying, don't come and see me. It was a nasty thing to say on TV. She didn't say anything bad, she just said we're not together.'

'What's the deal now then?' Dane interjected. 'Are you together now or not?'

Indeed, Vinnie appeared to feel that Alex needed a bit of tutoring in the ways of the media (although in truth, Katie was more than capable of giving him a masterclass). Alex mentioned an interview he'd done with *OK!* magazine, in which he'd said that he was 'very gay' as in 'very happy'. Vinnie did not approve. 'If you're not gay, why are you saying that?' he demanded.

'It's two steps forward, then ten steps back with you,' Stephen cut in. 'Don't say stupid stuff. As much as you're saying they [the media] are writing stuff about you, you're giving them the ammunition, you become the laugh.'

'Alex, it does seem like you enjoy your gay headlines and cross-dressing headlines,' said Heidi. 'It does, from a layman's perspective.'

Vinnie went on: 'I think you are playing up to it. You've created a character that isn't you.'

'You are a fricking tossed salad,' said Stephen. 'You need to decide what you want to be and be that thing.'

Vinnie wasn't the only one to express his concern, either. Heidi also had reservations about Alex's relationship with Katie. 'There's tons of women out there,' she told him. 'Are you with her because she's famous? Why you gonna pick someone with all that baggage unless she's famous? It looks like she bounces from dude to dude, to dude. She dumped that dude [Pete] that everyone loves.'

But it wasn't like that, insisted Alex: Katie accepted him for who he was. After that, he became more serious still: 'I'd die for her,' he said. 'I'd put my life down for her.'

'You feel that way after six months?' said a surprised-sounding Heidi. 'Wow, you like her a lot!'

Alex then went on to admit something that had not been made public before – that he and Katie were to all intents and purposes living together. This really was a serious relationship, then – and one that was becoming more so all the time.

Alex and Vinnie went out to work out in the garden together (Vinnie may not have wanted to appear in a film with Alex, but he was certainly happy to extend the hand of friendship.) Heidi watched them with a dreamy look. 'Vinnie is so hot,' she said. 'His wife is beautiful, too. I've seen pictures. He's so hot – he's awesome, he's so cool. He looks cool, he acts cool.' Clearly she had a crush.

Other sides to Alex were coming out, too. Stephen was a born-again Christian and often engaged his fellow housemates in conversations about religion. Now he did so with Alex, with whom he also said a prayer, asking him to repeat: 'Father Lord, tonight with my friend Stephen, I'm asking you to come into my life.'

'I'm willing to believe,' said Alex.

'God has a plan for you, brother,' Stephen told him. 'Here's what I know. He wants to reveal it to you – show it to you.'

In the meantime, the knives were out for Jonas and Katia again. Katia appeared to have put a stop to their romance, before it was all back on again, a ploy some of the housemates believed was just an attempt to escape eviction (Katia, along with Heidi and Lady Sovereign, was up for the chop).

'She's had a think about it and thought, that's how I can stay in again,' said Vinnie.

'She's just a user,' declared Stephanie. 'He's very immature. He's just a twenty-five-year-old mummy's boy. I want to get rid of Sov and the rest of the farting classes.'

In fact, Katia and Sov were not doing a great deal to endear themselves to the rest of the household. Sov had hidden a tin of corned beef that she'd stolen from the other housemates, further irritating Vinnie and Stephanie, who reiterated that she was not a 'team player'. Katia then refused to do the washing up, telling Sov: 'I'm not doing the washing up, it'll take me forever.'

It was Alex who correctly identified what was going on. 'There's Stephen, Vinnie, Ivana and Stephanie in one camp; me, Jonas, Nicola, Dane in the middle, and Sov and Katia on the far side,' he said. 'I'm not impressed with the younger girls not helping out. Maybe it's the arrogance of youth? The older guys are not as tolerant as me. The younger people in here don't realise there's a power struggle.'

Outside the house, life went on and Katie was forced to sit and take it while all the housemates appeared to advise Alex to dump her. No one was more aware of the vagaries of reality TV than she, but even so, it wasn't much fun. She was feeling 'very low,' she told her immediate circle, with one friend adding, 'She is already missing her man so much. Now she has to sit there while they all slag her off.'

Pete was paying no attention to what was going on: he was pictured beaming with Junior and Princess as he took them out for breakfast, still adamant there was no other woman in his life: 'I haven't chatted up girls since I was twenty-two, and I'm thirty-six now,' he admitted. 'I just don't know what to say to someone – I'm more shy now to approach someone than I was back then because I'm older, so I wouldn't know what to say. Someone would have to slap me in the face with a chat-up line to get it.'

Katie, meanwhile, was pictured at the première of the stage show *Legally Blonde* on 15 January, heading out the next night to Danielle Lloyd's engagement party – the model was to marry Jamie O'Hara. That didn't go according to plan, either: Danielle was wearing a £26,000 Swarovski crystal encrusted gown, which was so lovely that someone else present had already worn it – Katie. She chose it to attend the civil ceremony of Gary Cockerill and Phill Turner the previous August, something she rather tactlessly told Danielle, who was said to be in tears. Nor would Katie pose for pictures with her – she was clearly in a foul mood.

In the aftermath, a spokesperson for Danielle denied there had been any tensions between the pair. 'Danielle and Katie are best friends, there's no truth in the matter,' he declared. 'They are completely different dresses. They're by the same designer, but they're not the same dress.'

At least Danielle rounded things off in a way that played down any negative aspects to it all: '*I had the best night*,' she said on Twitter. '*Thank you to everyone who came. We had the night of our lives.*'

It might have taken Katie's mind off the negative comments from inside the house, but only briefly: as if all the *Big Brother* abuse were not enough, she also had to deal with a lot of venom, courtesy of Twitter postings, too. Indeed, it got so bad that at times, Katie was tempted to stop twittering altogether.

'Kate is a tough cookie and she's grown used to what she calls "the haters", who are constantly taking pops at her,' revealed a source. 'But the level of abuse on Twitter can be intolerable. She really is in two minds about staying on the site. She gets lots of really lovely messages from her true fans, who look up to her and they are an absolute pleasure, but in the same breath, there are the mindless idiots who bombard her with crude, abusive comments – which are there for all the public to see. She tries to ignore it, but it's hard not to be upset. She is considering all her options. It's sad, but that's what happens when you're in the public eye. Kate is trying to rise above it.'

Everyone, it seemed, was having a go at everyone else. Michelle Heaton, who was one of Katie's closest friends and therefore could normally be relied upon to toe the party line, was pretty tactless: 'Katie can do better than Alex,' she said on *Big Brother's Little Brother*. 'He's a lovely guy, but she can do better.'

Katie herself seemed perfectly happy, however, with the man she had. Rather boldly, Alex had announced to his fellow housemates that their relationship began within hours of meeting on 17 July 2009: it was, 'straight back to her house the first night,' he declared, adding, 'A good night, though!' Katie, however, was not annoyed: she took to Twitter to reassure everyone that all was well. '*Absence makes the heart grow fonder*,' she tweeted. '*Our relationship goes beyond* Big Brother: *I'll be waiting with open arms*.'

Back in the house, Alex's revelations were greeted with some good-natured nudging. Dane laughed it off, while Vinnie scolded him, saying he would be in trouble for sharing that one with the world. Dane, meanwhile, appeared to be finding the situation he was in, namely living at close quarters with his ex-girlfriend's current beau, a little odd: Katie, he told Vinnie, wasn't as famous as she'd been a decade earlier when she'd dated him. (That, incidentally, was a moot point. In 2000,

Katie had been little more than a glamour model, albeit a well known one; these days she was one of the most famous women in Britain, and if she kept earning at her current rate, would soon be one of the richest, as well.)

Katie looked pretty, 'until she opened her mouth,' Vinnie replied.

'She'd come out with some stupid shit,' confided Dane.

'He's gonna get absolutely chewed up,' said Vinnie, adding that Alex was a 'loveable prat.'

'She didn't want him coming in here,' said Dane, almost certainly incorrectly. Then finally, he came out with something that the viewers had suspected all along: 'I find it hard talking about Kate in front of Alex,' he said. 'It's weird we have both been with the same girl.'

The evictions had begun: the first to go were Katia and Heidi – Alex, incidentally, had not once been put up for eviction, as the public were clearly enjoying him far too much. Now Lady Sovereign once again faced the chop, this time up against Nicola T (the public seemed to share the view that it was the youngest housemates who were the most annoying).

Alex had started to drop hints that he was planning to propose to Katie one day soon (shopping for Katie was 'stressful' he said, because she can, 'buy the whole shop'), although he certainly didn't seem to mind when Nicola T was given a chore which involved her first insulting and then giving a kiss to her housemates. Nicola seemed to like him, too: 'He is one of the nicest guys I have ever met in my life,' she said. 'So kind, so friendly, dozy. He is such a decent guy – such a good soul. He's literally a Labrador.'

Another task involved both Nicola T and Ivana stripping down to their underwear to pose for the housemates as they drew sketches: Dane walked off with the first prize. Alex was on the receiving end of some teasing: it had been noted that Ivana seemed to think he was pretty attractive, too.

The *Big Brother* producers continued to play psychological tricks: sugar in the kitchen was swapped with salt (something the celebrities were not told about until they'd made their morning cups of tea), the opulent furnishings were taken away and the bed sheets replaced with hessian. Alex continued to talk about Katie and Pete, despite the dire warnings from all quarters that Katie would make him pay for this: Pete 'seems a good geezer,' said Vinnie, adding that Alex should, 'put out the olive branch.'

'He's Saint Pete and she's the Devil,' sighed Alex, adding, 'I've heard he's all right with me. I can totally understand how he must feel.'

Outside the house, Pete announced that his new album, *Unconditional: Love Songs*, would be out shortly: '*I am releasing my love album on February 1st just in time for Valentine's Day,'* he tweeted. *'It's got five soul classics and a compilation of love songs I've recorded over the last 15 years including an awesome duet with Brian McKnight. At dance rehearsals for tour. Sean Cheeseman is an amazing choreographer. Just been auditioning the band for my tour. These guys are awesome. And the dancers ... Omg I've got some work to do. Sharp sharp sharp.'*

Back in the house, Stephen and Sisqo were evicted, much to the delight of Vinnie, who declared the two who went against his leadership had, 'both bitten the dust.'

Outside, Katie was said to be considering her future. Recently, she had attended the television awards, where she had been booed by the crowd, and according to some sources, was thinking of putting the Jordan persona well and truly back in the closet and emerging simply as Katie Price.

'Katie was really taken aback by all the booing she received at the television awards last week,' said one. 'She has been thinking for a while about how she can "cleanse her soul" and win back some of her lost popularity. She transformed herself from Jordan into celebrity wife and mother Katie Price, but since her split from Peter Andre last May, Katie seems to have gone back to the old Jordan – falling out of nightclubs drunk and flashing her breasts at photographers. Katie met a couple of spiritual advisers – an older man in his 50s and a woman in her 40s. They began to give Katie advice about finding her true self, and putting the problems and behaviour associated with being Jordan behind her.

'She's even talking about visiting the great holy sites of the East, including the temples of India and China. And she also fancies a bathe in the Hindu holy river, the Ganges. She is looking at spiritualism as a chance to cast the impurities out of her life and find inner peace.'

If so, it didn't last for long. Without Alex to help her bear the strain, Katie seemed to be finding it difficult to cope with matters relating to Pete, and for the first time in months, she appeared to lose it as far as he was concerned. She turned up at his house unannounced – usually any meetings were carried out with military efficiency – while he was actually away from home and appeared to lose control.

'Katie just showed up unannounced,' said a witness to the scene. 'She was mad and manic, and kept screaming: "Where's Pete?" I don't know what it was about – just that it wasn't about their children, who were with Pete by prior agreement. But she should not have turned up like that without an appointment. And when they told her he wasn't there, she demanded they let her in to check. Someone got Pete on the phone to tell him what was going on, and he ordered the staff to get rid of her.

'She has become the ex from hell. She cannot accept their relationship is over – she has to do things like this to grab his attention. Katie thinks everything is going wrong and blames Pete. She realises her life was better when they were together, and even now thinks everything would be all right again if they reconciled. Pete hasn't found anyone else yet, so Katie cannot see why he doesn't want her but he won't speak to her on the phone.'

Had Alex been with her, he might have been able to calm her down. According to some friends, there was trouble there, too: Katie was potentially viewing him as competition, something that totally destroyed her relationship with Pete, and she had very mixed feelings about what was going on in the show.

'Katie has been watching all of the show – even the live feeds – and is furious,' revealed a friend. 'Even though he has only said nice things, Katie has been complaining about Alex trading off her fame. She thinks he is hogging the limelight – she hates the idea that the public is seeing Alex without her.

'Katie is so jealous she is even worried about how popular he has become. She saw Peter become "Saint Peter" after they broke up – now she is worried when she and Alex split up that he will become "Saint Alex". She is still annoyed he broke a promise not to talk about their relationship on the show, and she's talking about dumping him when he's voted out.'

No one was really sure what Katie would do when

Alex came out, probably not even Katie herself, but she did want to play down the incident at Pete's house: 'Katie did go round to Pete's on Monday, but it was to pick up a passport for Princess Tiammii,' said her spokesman. 'She was going to Manchester on Tuesday and she needed ID, which Pete had, for Tiammii for the flight to Manchester.'

In the house, Alex's confessions were becoming more lurid: he once enjoyed an orgy with five women, he said, but didn't remember it until he was shown the photographic evidence (Dane had just confessed to a session with six women at once). Dane also replaced Vinnie as the favourite to win at the bookies: he himself was beginning to elaborate on the real reason for his split with Katie: it was, apparently, because she would not stop doing naked shots.

'[It was] lots of little things, really,' he said. 'If you hear her side of things it was because of Victoria [Beckham], I was working too hard with Victoria. [But] at the time I was quite jealous. She stopped doing all the nudie shots, the really naughty things. Then she did one just to spite me and I said, "If you do it, I'll leave you," and she did it. We were together two and a half years – it was quite substantial, really.'

Nor could Dane resist bringing up the subject of the sex tape that the two of them had made together, which somehow found its way onto the Internet and caused a huge ruckus at the time. 'I think someone sent that to me a while ago, that tape,' said Vinnie.

In many ways, Dane seemed as obsessed as his ex when it came to who was the more famous. 'At the time when it came out it was us [Another Level] that were big, it made her a lot bigger; it's what set her up,' he declared. As for the sex tape, it was not only more searched than Pamela Anderson's, but 'the biggest thing on the Internet.'

But that had been a decade ago, and Katie had certainly moved on. So just what was she planning next?

CHAPTER 10

ALL TO PLAY FOR

There was less than a week of *Big Brother* to go. It was still not entirely clear who the ultimate winner would be, although Dane remained favourite at this point, but there were still more chores to get through. And by this stage, the remaining housemates wanted to impress. They had all entered the house for their various reasons, whether it was to promote their careers, revive interest in them or simply to show the public what they were really like and now, as the end neared, the stakes were getting higher. Who would make it through to the very end?

Ivana Trump proved to be a very good sport when she was made the subject of an elaborate hoax, in the course of which she was told that she had won Best

International Businesswoman on a Reality TV Show award from *Kugel Fresh* (in fact, the Scandinavian magazine did not exist and there was a very good chance that Ivana realised that, too). Indeed, given the way events played out, there's a very good chance that she had worked out what was going on, right from the start.

Ivana was given her award – a glass vase on a wooden plinth – and cried, 'I won! I won! Martha Stewart must be fuming by now!'

Stephanie asked to see it, took it and, as she had been instructed to, immediately dropped it so the award smashed. 'It smashed in my hand,' she said, as she began to cry and apologise to Ivana at the same time (although the tears continued when she got to the Diary Room – the strain was beginning to show).

'It's OK, it happens,' said Ivana briskly. 'Now the task is to put it together. How about I have a crazy go and Big Brother will give us crazy glue?'

But Big Brother had other ideas: Ivana was taken to the Task Room, where she was told there was a video link-up for her to make an acceptance speech.

'Good afternoon, ladies and gentleman, my friends, my fans,' she said. 'I would like to thank you so much for this wonderful award. I'm really deeply honoured and overwhelmed. I'd also like to thank *Celebrity Big Brother* in [the] UK for having me on the show and giving me [this] fantastic opportunity, and of course

[the] Swedish television show, which is called *Kugel Fresh*, for choosing me and nominating me, and giving me this prestigious award. Thank you so much.'

This was followed by a few words in German and Russian, after which Ivana was told to wind up: 'We have to move on? OK,' said Ivana. 'For the European viewers again, I'm very honoured. It is a category in business and a combination of the beauty brains. I might be blonde, but I'm quite bright and have achieved quite a bit, and I'm very proud of what I have done. My biggest accomplishment is my three children and I already have grandchildren, and they cannot call me grandma, they have to call me Ivana-ma. And I have a nice life and I have been on a television show in UK, on *Celebrity Big Brother*. Now, going to the third week, it has been really, for me, an incredible challenge and I'm enjoying myself. Thank you so much, I love you.'

The others laughed as they watched the speech transmitted to them, but it's a moot point whether any of them could manage a few words in German or Russian. Besides, Ivana had been a very good sport. The housemates were given a celebration dinner, to be attended in full evening dress, in the course of which they all had to give each other awards: Jonas was the Least Famous Housemate, Vinnie was the Most Famous Housemate and Nicola was awarded Most Attractive Housemate. Stephanie was a little upset: she got the

Bitchiest Housemate trophy. But all in all, the episode proved to be an entertaining one: this *Big Brother* was turning out to be a big success.

Alex was proving a pretty good sport, too. He stripped to the buff in the *Big Brother* bathroom to enable Jonas and Nicola T to spray him with fake tan: Dane and Vinnie were in hoots of laughter as they watched. 'What will your girlfriend think, mate?' asked Jonas, as he sprayed Alex's back.

'Forget the girlfriend! What do you think the rest of the nation's gonna think?' Alex demanded.

He then protected his modesty with a towel as Nicola manoeuvred the tan in the trickier areas around his behind: 'Is there any space?' asked Vinnie. This was just one of a few episodes during which Alex's standing in the public eye rocketed: he simply refused point-blank to take himself seriously, just got on with the various ludicrous tasks set him and didn't have a bad word to say about anyone. It was beginning to seem that Katie was quite right to suggest that he should appear on the show to illustrate to the public what he was really like.

In truth, it was Vinnie's image that was beginning to suffer on the show. Although at the outset he had been the straightforward favourite to win, more recently he appeared to adopt a more bullying demeanour and he did himself no favours at all when he told Ivana that they had all laughed as they watched her make her acceptance speech. It made him appear bullying, almost cruel. He had been an extremely bossy member of the household, very much feeling that he could order the others about to get his own way, and this was not only resented by some members of the Big Brother household: it wasn't playing too well on the outside, either.

Strangely, it was beginning to seem as if the one person capable of standing up to him was none other than Alex. Vinnie made a rather snide remark to the effect that Alex clearly owned a dinner suit for when he was, 'doing the doors,' a jibe Alex was remarkably cool about. He was making himself look bad, and it had not gone unnoticed that when, a couple of days earlier, Vinnie challenged Alex to a fight, saying Alex could throw the first punch, Alex had responded that it would be like, 'hitting your granddad.' There was a subtle shift in power in the house and although the housemates themselves might not have been aware of this, it was certainly noticeable to the viewers outside.

Indeed, having started with odds at 50-1, Alex now leapfrogged into pole position to win the show. 'Alex would win hands down if the winner was crowned for entertainment and his popularity is showing in our liabilities. He is the biggest gamble of the series and a terrible result, but easily the most deserving winner,' said Gary Burton, a spokesman for Coral. Katie should have been pleased: given that Alex was now unquestionably becoming one of the show's most popular participants, it seemed that the public was, after all, approving of her choice of partner.

The *Big Brother* producers wanted the show to go out with a bang and so they pulled out all the stops to ensure that end. Davina McCall had hosted the show for the whole of its ten-year history and now, for the first time ever, she was actually going to enter the house herself. Not that the housemates knew it: they were to be dressed up as animals, and so was Davina – as a chicken, in fact. She was, she said, 'Very, very nervous.' It was to be yet another episode that made for very good television and which was purportedly giving the show's producers food for thought about whether the programme might have the legs to go on for a few years yet.

And so, a total first: Davina was to enter the *Big Brother* house. Her introduction into the household slightly mirrored that of Ivana's, in that it involved a body switch. Nicola T went into the Diary Room dressed as a chicken and Davina came out in the self-same costume, but not before a briefing in the Diary Room.

'This is the best, thank you so much,' said Davina, sitting in the big chair. 'I'm very, very nervous. I'm shaking, I'm really frightened.' Nicola, meanwhile, was spirited away.

Big Brother spoke: Davina was to answer to the name

of Nicola, not to do anything to draw attention to herself and to remove her earpiece. 'Big Brother is always here,' BB continued.

'I've always wanted you to say that to me,' Davina replied.

And so she entered the house, but almost immediately the other contestants sussed that the chicken was not a Page 3 girl, but a stranger in their midst. The others, also dressed as animals, were only allowed to make animal noises but Vinnie, dressed as a horse, demurred, 'That's not Nic.'

'Definitely good call, Vinnie! Definitely good call,' said Dane.

'It might be Ivana,' suggested Vinnie. 'Nicola don't even walk like that – too tall as well.'

'Could it be Heidi?' asked Alex, who was dressed as a cockerel.

The animals began to circle Davina, with some joking that Alex thought it might be Katie. 'He thinks it's his missus,' said one.

Stephanie was the only woman left in the house and Davina sought shelter with her before being summoned back to the Diary Room. 'They are really spooked,' she said, adding that she thought they found Nicola's unannounced departure rather frightening. 'It was pretty menacing,' she went on. 'I never thought they'd feel threatened by a chicken.

'Alex and Vinnie were the scariest. The thing is, Vinnie's serious face is really serious, even when he has the horse's head on.'

Davina went back into the house, complete with chicken head, but the others were beginning to guess who she really was. 'If it's you, Davina, you're getting your butt kicked,' warned- Dane, and indeed it was, although mercifully no such outcome awaited the presenter. Instead, as she removed her head, everyone laughed and hugged her: 'This has been the best night of my life,' Davina told them, before wishing them luck and disappearing again.

It had all gone very well and somehow illustrated why, at its best, *Celebrity Big Brother* worked. The oddity of this house, in which inhabitants could be spirited away with no one noticing, and which had a talking tree in the sitting room, added to a sense of unreality, an atmosphere that its famous inhabitants somehow had to puzzle through as they tried to work out what was really going on. Then there was the inspired silliness of putting everyone in animal costumes and the fact that these costumes rendered their wearers somehow frightening: whoever would have thought that anyone could be unnerved by a man dressed up as a horse? At best, there is always a feeling of being one step away from anarchy in *Big Brother*, the constant threat of falling over the edge. When it happened, of course, that created a whole new set of problems, but this was one episode in which everything stayed just the right side of harmonious – but with a decidedly malevolent edge.

Vinnie's reputation had taken a bit of a hit during his time in the house and the producers clearly thought it would be a good idea to play on this. Earlier in the day, the Tree of Temptation had given him a new task, for which he would be rewarded by being able to watch a match between Leeds and Tottenham Hotspur, but this would certainly mean that he had to swallow his manly pride: he would have to admit to Alex that he enjoyed cross-dressing before shedding a few tears at the thought of leaving the house.

He had to 'confess he's made some really great mates,' the tree told him, adding that he should tell Alex that the experience could provide him with the opportunity to 'get you on the telly' or perhaps the lead role in a romantic comedy. Vinnie protested at first, but was ultimately resigned to his fate.

And so it was that shortly afterwards, Vinnie took Alex aside. 'A few years ago,' he confessed, 'I did it, sort of out with the lads. I thought it was all right – nothing wrong with it,' he continued, adding that he had 'quite liked it. What goes on in your bedroom is your own thing.'

'Exactly,' said Alex seriously.

'Especially if you get a decent bit of gear,' Vinnie went on.

Over lunch, Vinnie became maudlin. Would they all keep in touch, he asked the other housemates. They had become such good friends.

'You're not getting all soppy, are you?' laughed Alex. Visibly upset, Vinnie moved to the bedroom.

'He must be a really good actor,' said Nicola. 'If that wasn't real, he's really good.' It was really good, too – and at least Vinnie had been given the chance to show that he could be sensitive, too.

As the show neared its climax, the odds-on favourites to win were none other than Katie's two exes, Alex and Dane. Both had shown themselves to be good sports and the public appeared to approve of Katie's taste in men – she had just been pictured having lunch with Dane's parents. And that little spat at the New Year's Eve party was now a thing of the past. It wasn't put on, either: after initial fears about how they would all get on, Alex and Dane appeared to have formed a genuine bond.

Katie was proud of her men: 'I love *BB*, but when you know somebody really closely, it's a different kind of viewing,' she said of Alex. 'He has been himself and I know no different. He is good fun. Dane is also doing very well.'

As she had been evicted from the house a day or two

earlier, Ivana echoed those sentiments. 'I like Alex – he's down to earth, has a very good heart and we were friends because I appreciated his dedication to exercise,' she said. 'Dane is a nice guy.'

The public clearly thought so, too. The winners were finally announced: Alex came first with 65.9 per cent of the public vote, Dane followed with 34 per cent and then Vinnie, Jonas and Stephanie. The show had been a spectacular success, so much so that there was even speculation that this would not be the last series after all. Channel 4 stated publicly that it was not looking to reverse its decision that this would be the last-ever *Celebrity Big Brother*, but there was a distinct possibility that Channel 5 might pick it up. After some initial derision, the show had ultimately proved its worth.

Alex was clearly delighted by events: 'I'm very overwhelmed. What an amazing, fantastic start to a New Year!' he told Davina, as he came out of the house – the declared winner – to a good deal of cheering in the background. His image had been turned around: the public was now beginning to think that, just as she had done with Pete, Katie had got herself a genuinely nice guy.

CHAPTER 11

FIRST PRIZE GOES TO...

Alex was cock-a-hoop: against all expectations, he'd won *Celebrity Big Brother*. He'd proven himself in the public eye, too. And he could not have been more generous about the people with whom he'd spent the last three weeks. 'Vinnie has been very inspirational to me,' he said. 'He's transitioned from athlete to actor, which is what I want to do. I'm not getting booed now. That's amazing... I'm speechless. My whole agenda in here was to be myself.'

He had, of course, been booed when he went into the show, and still got a taste of it when Davina brought up Katie's name. 'Come on, guys, don't do that,' said Alex serenely. 'I'm sorry guys, I'm not sorry, I really love Katie Price.' It was a brave thing to say, given Katie's penchant for dumping her menfolk on live television, but the lady herself seemed delighted by what had gone on.

That other unlikely outcome of the time in the house was that Alex and Dane appeared to have become friends. 'I was surprised by what a cool dude Dane is,' Alex admitted. 'I'm really looking forward to seeing more of Dane.'

Those sentiments were returned in full: 'I'm very, very happy that Alex won,' said Dane. 'The best line I've ever heard about him is he's a loveable prat – he's his own man, he's a gentleman. The first week I thought he was a Doris, but he's OK. He's a good lad.'

Vinnie was equally fulsome. 'I really feel for the fellow because he got the biggest boos going in, and hopefully he will get the biggest cheers coming out,' he said. 'I gave him a lot of banter. I've taught him everything I know, so hopefully he will win his next fight and hopefully, you lot will go and watch him.'

In all, the show ended on a very good-natured note, with a bit of a love fest between all the participants. 'This has been an emotional rollercoaster for me: I came in here with a lot of misconceptions in the press about me,' said Alex. 'I was quite naïve, but have listened to things you [Vinnie and Stephanie] and Stephen have told me, and I've taken on board things you've said to me.'

'I've grown a lot in this house and learnt a lot of lessons,' said Jonas.

Vinnie was delighted to have made it to the final: 'I thought I was gonna be gone after a week. It's been a wonderful experience and it's one we'll look back on,' he declared.

Stephanie had enjoyed herself, too. Despite the fact that she was a glamour puss of the first order, her last couple of days had seen her as an honorary bloke, and she had risen to the challenge with grace. 'Never been teased so much since I was ten,' she said. 'I laughed like a child, I felt like a child. You've been like teasing brothers. I think of the woman who walked in as a very stuck-up cow rather than the very shambly figure that's going to walk out.'

Indeed, Stephanie was the last woman left in the house and as such, became one of the boys for a while. 'They've just treated me like one of the gang. I've been doing a little bit of boxing. There's no telephone and I had to give up control, and that's something I find extraordinary. It was heaven!'

But she had also forged a warm bond with Ivana – 'We're elegant women of a certain age,' she said. 'We got up at six o'clock every morning.' In other words, both had iron self-discipline, which is how the two ended up leading such glamorous lives. As for that Bitchiest Housemate award – 'I came in here to show everyone I was a silly person and not a big bitch,' Stephanie said. 'Without Vinnie, there would have been no order. Dad was needed. Nic and I had a lovely time – she likes bows and girlie things.'

As for Jonas, there had been intense speculation as to whether he and Katia had a future together on the outside. It appeared they did not. 'I've never laughed so much in my life,' said Jonas, before turning to the subject of Katia: 'Let's just say that I'm over it. There's a lot of beautiful girls out there. I'm going to party tonight, who wants to come with me? I'm completely over it. It's hard to know if it's love or not, especially being caught up in the house; it felt more intense in there. But I'm over it now, I'm OK. But I did touch "bass" and I did do some hunting.'

He was shown a newspaper headline in which Katia declared that she loved Jonas: 'Too late baby!' was his response.

Of course, despite public assurances that she was rooting for him, Alex could not be totally sure of the reaction that he would get from Katie. She did have form: there had been that public dumping in the past, to say nothing of the fact that Katie did not enjoy being overshadowed by her partners. In the past few weeks, Alex's public profile had rocketed: while he had achieved some level of recognition when he first started dating Katie, it was nothing like what he'd got now. In fact, if he played his cards right, there was a good chance that, like his girlfriend, he could end up a household name.

So there was some speculation about what Katie's reaction would be when they were finally reunited. But all was well, with no threat that they were about to split up.

'He's the love of my life and he knows that,' she declared on *Big Brother's Big Mouth*, before adding how pleased she was that her current beau and her ex had ended up as the two finalists. 'The two guys I've been with have been the last two,' she pointed out. 'They are genuine guys, I don't go for shitheads!'

In the end, it was very much love and kisses all round. Alex admitted the odd doubt about his lady love had crossed his mind, but it had all turned out fine. 'Missing Katie was the hardest thing,' he said. 'When you get all that thinking time, I was thinking, is she going to be waiting for me when I come out? It's silly, it's a normal human reaction: I knew, deep down, she would be and the proof is in the pudding.'

He now wanted to build bridges with everyone and that included Pete. 'I'd like nothing more than to meet up with him and clear the air – because there are children involved it makes sense,' he said. 'I've got nothing against him: he's a good dad.' In truth, though, this was unlikely to happen. Given how reluctant Pete was to meet up with Katie, he would hardly likely to wish to spend time chatting with Alex, although he was prepared to be very open about the situation they all found themselves in. It was also the case that, although it wasn't known about at the time, Pete himself was indulging in a little fling, of which more anon.

Now that Alex was out of the house, it was back to business as usual. Ever the astute businesswoman, Katie was still taking a look at the various business deals that came her way, and one suggestion was that she might establish a boutique hotel. Given that she had done so much in the lifestyle market, it made a sort of sense.

'Now that the recession is supposedly over, she has been advised that property is becoming a more stable investment,' revealed a friend. 'After splitting from Peter Andre she felt the pinch, and her accountant called her in to have a chat about her finances. Katie is always in and out of London, staying at the Mayfair Hotel, but she said if she had her own then it could be more like a home from home. Katie knows her limitations, she doesn't want anything massive. She just wants a small boutique hotel that she can feel comfortable in and have some privacy.'

If she was going to do it, though, the hotel would have to be in Katie's trademark style and there was no telling what potential guests would make of that. 'You can just imagine what the rooms will look like,' the friend continued. 'It will be top-to-toe in pink with fluffy carpets and pink flowery drapes; it will be like the Playboy mansion on crack. You could have breakfast in the Botox Lounge, or supper in the Spraytan Room. And you'd better bring a pink tutu for karaoke in the bar. Michelle Heaton, Danielle Lloyd and her hairdresser pals Gary Cockerill and Phill Turner will practically move in with any other Z-lister who wants to be seen. For the amount of fans Katie still has, this could be a surprise moneyspinner – if guests can handle staying there among the dramas.'

And the dramas looked set to continue, no doubt about that. Pete reminded everyone that he was still around when he made public his plans for Valentine's Day: 'As far as Valentine's Day is concerned, Pete's special lady will be Princess,' said a friend. 'He's just too busy to be thinking about love at the moment. During the day he has custody of the kids and will do something special with them – they'll probably bake special cupcakes as it's Valentine's Day. After that he will be doing a presenting spot backstage at the BRIT Awards.' There was no mention of his ex.

His ex, however, was planning some romantic entanglements of her own. In the wake of Alex's *Big Brother* triumph, the duo was now firmly established as a couple and both had publicly declared their love for one another. And it seemed that matters were about to get more serious still. 'This year I will marry Alex and I'm going to have his kids,' Katie told *OK!* magazine, before making a very direct dig at her ex: 'I wish I'd met Alex six years ago. He's perfect in every way.' And children, 'two or three' according to Alex, were also on the cards: 'I've always said I want a big family,' Katie announced.

Alex was thrilled. First, he had been announced as the winner of *Celebrity Big Brother* and now this – it was all too much. 'It's been a fantastic start to the New Year and it's going to be even more fantastic now this is happening,' he said. 'I actually asked Katie to marry me after my fight in September, so it's something we've been discussing for some time. I hope the public learns something from this. Four weeks ago I was the bad guy getting booed, now they're cheering me. They got it wrong about me, and they've got it wrong about Katie.'

This was all quite a step forward, especially as it hadn't been that long since Katie had publicly dumped him (two months ago) and considered doing so again (just two weeks ago). But she had made up her mind: Alex was to be her new consort, to take over from Pete and become the new male half of the country's most famous celebrity couple.

'It's a huge turnaround from a few months ago, but now Katie has decided her future does lie with Alex,' revealed a friend. 'He was a big – and surprise – success on *Celebrity Big Brother*. Katie had her doubts as to how she would react to him on a reality TV show, but she found that it actually made her fonder of him. Now she wants to tell the world she is going to marry Alex and she doesn't want to wait too long to wed. She wants to do it this year. Katie saw a different side to Alex on *Celebrity Big Brother*. Now, they are happier than they've ever been and she's determined to marry again.'

They certainly seemed to be getting on just fine: Alex allowed it to be known that in the wake of the *Big Brother* win, they'd spent a passionate night together. Having babies was certainly going to be on the horizon soon.

'Alex was so horny he basically pounced on Katie as soon as he could,' said a friend. 'They headed straight to her dressing room and spent twenty minutes alone, getting to know each other again. Producers on *Big Brother's Big Mouth* were worried they wouldn't be out in time to film the show late on Friday. One walked in on them and Katie shouted, "Pervert!" After that, they went back to their home.

'They didn't get much sleep before they headed to a plush health spa together. They talked about having a summer wedding. He even practised carrying her over the threshold!'

Alex was certainly full of plans. Not only did he want to get married, but he was looking forward to the next stage of his working life, too. 'I'd love to go to

Hollywood and get a career out there,' he said excitedly. 'I think it's totally amazing that Stephen and Vinnie have said they will help me. I still have a fight in three months, so I am focusing on that at the moment, but in the back of my mind, I'm thinking I am an actor!' But above all else, of course, he was thinking about getting wed.

Pete was, as yet, silent on the subject, although the usual rows raged on in the background about all their plans. Katie and Alex decided that they would have a surprise last-minute holiday, which meant more kerfuffle about who was doing what with the children: 'Pete dropped the kids off at school as agreed on Monday morning,' a friend of Pete related. 'He has had them since Wednesday so Kate could have her weekend with Alex. Kate was meant to pick them up after school yesterday, but word filtered back she was on her way to Heathrow and the nannies would be looking after the kids. Pete hit the roof!'

Meanwhile, Alex was being a little coy: asked if he would make a romantic proposal, he replied, 'I've got lots of plans, but I'm going to keep them a mystery. You'll have to keep guessing. I've completely realised how fantastic she is. How generous and kind she is, and how much I fancy her. She is just the perfect woman for me.' He was feeling broody, he said. What was the point in holding back?

So, the couple set off on their impromptu holiday to discuss future plans – and the date and the location? Las Vegas, February 2010.

CHAPTER 12

PETE SPEAKS OUT

With the romance playing out across the nation's media, and there was no doubt that many were gripped by it, one person had not said a great deal and that person was Pete. There were the numerous spats about childcare, as usual, and a great deal of ill-tempered comment about the trivial aspects of life, but Pete had not gone into much detail about what his own feelings were at this time over the actual cause of the break-up, although he had, of course, spoken about his relationship with the children.

But that was about to change: perhaps now that he saw his ex-wife really was seriously involved with another man, he felt this was a good time to reveal the real reason why the couple divorced – or perhaps it was just that he'd calmed down, come to terms with it all and felt that it would be therapeutic to get it off his chest. At any rate, something had been welling up inside of him and he had to let it out.

For a start, he was feeling much calmer, more at ease with himself and extremely rested after his two-week break. He might not have been able to take the children to Australia, but even so, the trip had given him time to sit back and assess what had been going on in his life. He had been so caught up in the story, the drama, the rivalry with his ex and now her new husband, that he had been in danger of forgetting who he was, and now he'd had a chance to re-establish his own identity, his own life.

'I'm happy in a way I haven't been since my twenties,' he told one interviewer. 'I spent two weeks in Australia at Christmas with my family and friends. I did nothing but relax, chat, go out for dinner, play backgammon with my dad and sit in the sun. I was away from everything, all the madness; I felt my identity returning to me. I accepted the end of my relationship a long time ago, but I found it hard to come to terms with the place that left me in. Now I'm finally happy in myself. I think I've found the real me.'

Clearly, the time spent in Australia had done him the world of good, so much so that he was now able to take a more rational view of the past. And so it proved that the real reason why the marriage had foundered was the one that everyone had suspected all along – that Katie had got too close to her riding instructor, Andrew Gould. There was no suggestion that the two had actually had an affair – like Katie, Andrew was married – but that Pete had become uncomfortable about the situation and despite his repeated requests that she should distance herself from him, Katie had refused to back down. Inevitably, matters came to a head.

Those with long memories would recall that what appeared to have triggered the split, all those months ago, was the publication of pictures of Katie partying with a group of friends and without Pete. The photos sparked a furore because they seemed to imply (correctly, as it turned out) that she and Pete were on the verge of leading separate lives, but the pictures also implied (incorrectly) that she might be having an affair. In essence, one of the group out with her that night was Andrew Gould and given that Pete had repeatedly asked Katie to stay clear, it was all too much.

'Ultimately, a marriage has to be about trust,' said Pete. 'Once that trust is gone... I would never ask her to stop riding, but I did ask her to move her horses or get a new instructor. She didn't. It was no secret among our friends that I was unhappy. When we weren't working, I always wanted us to have a family day with the kids. I'd wake up and she'd have left already to go riding. In

America she'd go out riding with no make-up, but here, she'd go out on her horse, fully made-up.'

What was emerging here was quite straightforward jealousy. Given her distress when the marriage finally and irrevocably foundered, in retrospect it seems odd that Katie didn't realise that she was pushing Pete too far, but that was, indeed, the case. She was used to getting her own way, in relationships as much as everything else, and Katie was being reckless in not listening more closely to what her husband was saying. But she didn't – and so the marriage broke up. What made it even odder was that Katie suffered from pangs of jealousy, too – and that when she asked Pete to behave differently for the sake of her own feelings, he'd been only too happy to comply.

The episode didn't just affect Katie, either. Andrew Gould was a well-respected dressage instructor and at the time there had been incredulity that he allowed himself to be drawn into the soap opera surrounding Katie's life. He was married to Polly and they had two children, Oliver and Louie, and when the story broke over six months previously, he had point-blank denied they were having an affair.

In the aftermath of the furore, Andrew and Polly gave an interview to the *Daily Telegraph*, which made it patently obvious that nothing was going on – for a start, Polly had been present on the night in question, but simply hadn't made it into the pictures. They had been as unprepared for the deluge of attention as anyone, for although they had been professionally involved with one of the country's most-photographed women for some time, neither had ever really taken on board what life was like on Planet Katie. They were in for a short, sharp shock.

'I woke up one morning to discover I had become what I think is known as a love rat,' said Andrew, who then held up one headline: 'JORDAN'S HANDSOME HORSEY PAL TELLS PETE: "MEET ME MAN TO MAN AND I'LL SAVE YOUR MARRIAGE"'. This was, as it turned out, something of a fabrication. 'The last thing I want to do is meet Pete face to face,' Andrew had said at the time. 'I got asked if I wanted to meet Pete and I replied: "I don't think Pete would want to talk to me." Astonishingly, that turned into a headline saying I want to see him, man to man.

'It was utterly unbelievable. We had eight car-loads of paparazzi outside the house. Even when I told them that Polly was there that night, they insisted they had looked at the club's CCTV and couldn't see her. On and on, it went. It just became more and more outrageous. If it hadn't been such a nightmare it would actually have been quite funny because none of it, not a word of it, was true. Yes, Polly and I are friends with Katie, but she is first and foremost, our business client.'

Matters really had got out of control. There had been stories that Andrew and Katie had been on trips out of the country together and had been spending a lot of time alone. In reality, this was a mixture of truth that had been misinterpreted as well as downright falsehood – which is why, some months after the event, Andrew and Polly decided to finally put on record the facts of the case.

'Yes, I've been on trips to Holland with her,' Andrew conceded. 'But I've taken all my clients when they want to buy new horses. Those four hours I was supposed to be "holed up in her house"? Polly was there for about three hours, I arrived for the last hour. When I drove out of Katie's gates, a million cameras flashed. When Polly drove out in her car a few seconds later, they all put their cameras down.'

Polly was having an equally torrid time of it. 'The worst thing was the emails,' she recalled. 'I was getting them from all sorts of people I'd never met, all telling me to kick Andrew out, that there is no smoke without fire. When we decided we were not going to give interviews, comments from us were just made up. We were just friends with Katie and she was, and remains, a valued client. We had absolutely no idea how out of hand the whole thing would become.'

But it did: for a time the public was convinced that Andrew was the reason for the break-up of the marriage and as it turned out, they were right. But what was really going on was not that Katie was having an affair – rather, she was ignoring the wishes of her husband and building up such reserves of resentment on his part that it would only be a matter of time before it all fell apart. Katie was used to getting her own way, but this time she pushed it too far. The Goulds' marriage survived, Katie and Pete's did not.

Months later, Pete was still clearly both furious and bitter about what had gone on. 'Let me make it clear I was totally faithful to her,' he declared. 'I never so much as held another girl's hand during our marriage. The vows we took meant everything to me. Once Katie was obsessed with a girl at my gym she thought fancied me, so I stopped going to the gym for three months, but she wouldn't switch riding instructors.'

It was a decision for which she was to pay a high price.

Nor, as it turned out, was the split as sudden as it seemed to the outside world. For a family man like Pete, walking out on his wife would have been a momentous decision and not one that would be taken on the spur of the moment. The problems had been building up for a long time. Almost a year before they finally parted, they had a short trial separation, during which Pete went to Cyprus for the best part of two weeks. 'I felt she didn't love me any more, but I was still determined to try to salvage things, make it work for us and for the kids,'

Pete related. 'We both had counselling. There were four things we both agreed to change and within two weeks, I had changed every single one. Kate didn't bother.'

A note of bitterness was creeping in. Pete had waited a long time before coming out with how he felt about it all, and now the full extent of his resentment towards his ex-wife was clear. Katie had become just too determined to have her own way – something that might have worked admirably as she built up her career, but it was no way to handle a relationship. The constant attention that the two were under was becoming too much, as well.

Pete had resolutely avoided as much of the circus surrounding the separation as he could have done, and made a point of not watching his ex-wife on *I'm A Celebrity*, too – an event Katie had said served merely to remind her constantly of Pete. Was this a last-ditch attempt to win him back? If so, it didn't work.

In fact, Katie rang Pete almost as soon as she emerged from the show. 'She asked me if I'd been watching,' said Pete. 'I genuinely hadn't seen any of it. Then she told me she was ending her relationship with Alex. I said that was up to her; all I was interested in talking to her about was the children. She wanted to see them, but they were supposed to be with me. I told her it was absolutely fine, I understood how important it was. I was trying to be a fair parent.'

It had been an open secret, too, that in the wake of the break-up, Katie bombarded Pete with texts and left messages for him on his voicemail, including one, according to some reports, of her singing 'I Will Always Love You' on the eve of the divorce. Pete was discreet about it, but it was clear that the reports were true. 'I don't want to say exactly what she said, I just assume she'd had a bit too much to drink,' he recounted.

Nor was there any prospect whatsoever of a reconciliation: matters had gone much too far for that. Quite apart from the presence of Alex on the scene, Pete had been made miserable by his marriage, with its constant power plays and jealousies, and even more miserable by the breakdown. He had no intention of putting himself through any of it again.

'I don't want to sound harsh, but I have to be clear,' he stated simply. 'I've been to hell and back, and I'm just recovering. That door is completely closed. I can absolutely say I will never go back. Ever.'

Indeed, he was finally able to feel that he could move on with his life (in fact, he'd already moved on a little further than he was publicly letting on, although he didn't feel ready to talk about that yet). 'I'm ready to think about someone else in my life,' he admitted. 'I do want to get married again, I do want to find someone else and I honestly would like to see Kate happy. I'd like her to find a man responsible enough to be a good influence on her and my children. If she met someone like that, I'd be happy. I don't know him [Alex], but it's about what's good for my children.'

That was, indeed, at the forefront of everyone's mind – but sorting out what they all agreed was in their best interests was easier said than done.

CHAPTER 13

A TALE OF TWO MEN

One of the many bones of contention between the trio was that Pete had never actually met Alex and appeared to have no wish to do so, either. But the fact was that Alex now played an increasing role in everyone's lives, and that included the children. Nor was he just Mum's boyfriend anymore: he was Mum's new husband, as far as the children were concerned, although the formalities had not yet come about at the time when Pete first spoke out about his feelings. Surely it was in everyone's best interests to get on speaking terms at some point soon?

Alex himself was certainly unafraid to weigh into the many controversies surrounding them all. Take the uproar about Princess's recent appearance with straightened hair and false eyelashes. He had been annoyed at all the fuss and said so, too. 'What mum doesn't dress up her little girl?' he demanded. 'Anyway, it wasn't even dressing up, just playing around with make-up. Princess was just sat on Kate's lap and said she wished she could have eyes just like mummy, and so they put the false lashes on her for a few minutes. It was a joke! It was disappointing that Pete called it "disgusting" in an interview.'

Disappointing or not, this statement would hardly get Pete onside. Alex, perhaps more than anyone, was keen to build bridges – 'Both Kate and I do still want to meet up with Pete at some point and sort everything out,' he said. But how could that be possible? Apart from anything else, if the three of them did meet up, it would be by its very nature two against one, even if Alex pulled out all the stops to stay neutral. But that would have been impossible, too: he was firmly on Team Katie, whether he approved of the label or not. Only when Pete himself found another partner could that aspect of it all be sorted out.

Meanwhile, Pete was beginning to think about looking for love again. He had been very public about the fact that he'd not been sleeping around: in the background he was, in fact, having a fling, but he just didn't feel able to own up to it yet. 'I'm looking forward to finding someone else,' he stated. 'I'm hoping it will just hit me like a ton of bricks. I'm a thirty-six-year-old man with children and I want someone who is prepared to take all of that on. I look at my parents, who have been together forever, and to me that is the ultimate success. That's what I want for myself, but it's all about the right girl. I want true love, a love that will last and a love I can trust.'

The above was said before Katie and Alex got married: now Pete would have to reassess everything fast. In the meantime, the honeymoon pair made plans. Katie was a genius at making money out of the media and Alex was learning fast, and so a business plan began to evolve, which everyone involved was hoping would net the happy couple a good £2 million, and actually started to take shape before the wedding ceremony itself.

'It's been carefully calculated,' revealed a source just before the two of them jetted off to Las Vegas. 'She's plotted with Alex's advisors over the last week. She wants to make as much money as possible and knows she needs to exploit her relationship with Alex to do that. The next one [photoshoot] is a holiday next week. Then there's something involving the kids. All of it was sorted without Alex's knowledge because he was in the house.' But chances are that he would have been more than happy to go along with it – this was now his life, too. And in fact, what Katie had actually been planning was as audacious as anything she'd ever been up to – for it was the wedding day itself.

And so they were wed, although they didn't have much time to spend together in the immediate aftermath of the nuptials. Katie jetted off to Vienna, where she appeared at the annual Vienna Opera Ball at the Vienna State Opera House, a very prestigious event to which she wore a baby-blue strapless gown teamed with diamonds. She was a guest of the Austrian entrepreneurs, Irene and Alexander Mayer: originally she had been asked to accompany the Austrian tycoon Richard Lugner, who took a celebrity date to the ball every year, but he had withdrawn his invitation after Katie broke his embargo, revealing she was accompanying him before his official announcement on 20 January.

Lugner made a habit of this: previous dates had included Nicolette Sheridan, Dita Von Teese, Paris Hilton, Raquel Welch and Sophia Loren. Katie was then replaced by Lindsay Lohan, who would have been paid $150,000, had she shown up. Instead she missed her flight, according to some accounts because she spent too long in the duty-free, which meant that Lugner was accompanied by his (much younger) girlfriend Anastasia 'Katzi' Sokol; it also meant that Katie had free rein at the ball as possibly the best-known woman there.

There was some mocking about the fact that Katie had been invited to such a top-notch event (the Austrian President Heinz Fischer was there, along with various minor members of European royalty), but in actual fact,

Vienna was exactly the sort of city that appealed to the less flashy aspects of Katie's life. It had a very famous riding school, which was very much up her street: 'I've heard a lot about what is probably the most important ball in Europe,' said Katie, who was very much on her best behaviour. 'I'm really looking forward to dancing the Viennese waltz with my friends and getting to know Austria. I'm an ambitious dressage rider and can't wait to see the Lipizzaner at Vienna's Spanish Riding School.' She acquitted herself well, too and the evening was deemed to be a great success.

There were, needless to say, already rumours about the state of the marriage but given the high profile of the couple, it would have been a miracle if nothing had been said. The two had barely seen one another, but that was unavoidable – both had schedules booked up for months in advance, and given the very last-minute aspect of the nuptials, the arrangements couldn't just be ignored.

Those rumours, according to Katie herself, were a 'joke'. 'If people really believe this, there has got to be something wrong,' she declared. 'It's a joke! People are treating me like a serial killer, I'm a villain. What have I actually done wrong? It [the wedding] was fantastic! We had a brilliant day, it was just like a dream.' She also reported that they had not, contrary to speculation, done a deal with a magazine and that she now intended to be known simply as Mrs Reid.

'I am in a happy place,' she went on. 'It's so great – New Year, new beginning and a new family life to start. We are so excited; me and Alex so want kids. We are trying, so let's hope, let's hope. I can't wait to get pregnant! I've grown up and learned a lot from my mistakes – and now I'm a Reidy! I want to be Reidinated! You won't see me out on the town for a very long time. It doesn't interest me.'

The fact that Alex was still out of the country – in India – was, of course, fuelling all the speculation, but this was a longstanding commitment that he had to honour, as detailed earlier in this book. And he didn't exactly calm matters down with an interview that he gave, implying, as it did, that his parents were seriously worried about what their son had done. But this was typically Alex – he spoke without really thinking about how what he said might come across. As Vinnie put it, he could sometimes be a 'loveable prat'.

'The wedding was whirlwind and a bit of a surprise,' he said. 'Katie planned it all. My mum and dad – my whole family, in fact – were a bit gutted. I managed to tell my mum in a quick call just minutes before, but no one else. I didn't get married for them, anyway. I got married for me, to make Alex Reid happy.'

It emerged that Katie had planned the wedding while Alex was still in the *Big Brother* house, with the help of her friends Gary Cockerill and Phill Turner. And the sniping was pretty much instantaneous, starting with reports that the ring he'd bought for his bride cost a mere £2,000. 'The stories saying that the ring I bought Katie only cost EUR 2,500 caused me a lot of trouble,' he revealed. 'She hit the roof. I can't say how much I paid, but it's more like EUR 68,000. You only get married once, don't you? And I wanted to push the boat out.'

The trip to India followed, which was all part of a documentary – *The Fight of His Life* – which would tell the story of Alex's bid to win a fight with the UK's current Middleweight Ultimate Challenge World Champion Tom 'Kong' Watson. But fatherhood beckoned, too. 'I'm a man in love and of course, I want children – lots – with my wife,' he declared. 'What red-blooded man wouldn't? And Katie's a great mum. I won't be back in time [for Valentine's Day] but you know me, I'm a tri-sexual. And I'll more than make up for it. Katie's got a very big surprise coming!'

And Alex certainly wasn't living the high life in the weeks immediately after his marriage. He was sleeping in a small fighters' dormitory in a village about 150 miles from Mumbai, and there were rumours that Katie wanted him to sack his own management and take up with the people who looked after her. 'Alex is a different person now,' said a friend. 'He can't see what is happening. He's besotted with Katie and just does anything she says. She'll bark orders down the phone at him, then send him a text saying, "I love you" and he'll fall for it.'

Meanwhile, Katie's former husband was still making his presence felt. A couple of years previously, Pete had suffered a very serious illness – meningitis – an unpleasant experience made significantly worse by the fact that rumours spread that he had died. Pete chose this moment to speak out about it: to some observers it almost seemed as if he was reminding everyone that he was still there, too.

'I completely freaked out,' he said, recalling the rumours. 'The thought that I could die from meningitis was in the back of my mind, but I certainly knew that I wasn't dead yet.

'It set my mind racing. Firstly, I worried that the doctors were not telling me something – that I was far more ill than they had led me to believe – and secondly, that my parents would have heard and been worried sick. I asked to speak to the doctor in charge of my case, who reassured me that if he had thought things were that serious, he would have had to tell me. So someone, possibly a hospital visitor or member of staff, must have started the rumour. But the psychological impact of hearing that I was supposed to be dead was something I would not wish on anyone.'

Meanwhile, Katie's new husband, Alex, was in a very

different frame of mind. He was relishing his new life: 'After this job I'm probably going to quit fighting for a bit,' he revealed. 'Work doesn't come first, Katie does. It's just been a mad few months. I've won *Big Brother* and got married. To Katie Price. Mad!'

He had other concerns, too. 'I put on nearly a stone in the *Big Brother* house,' he admitted. 'I'm fifteen stone now – that's almost three stone over my ideal fighting weight. I need to get fit again. I'm the heaviest I've ever been, and these Indian fighters are really pushing me hard. I'm on a diet now – a chicken curry diet.'

Alex refused to brood, though: it had been an amazingly eventful time and he was still mulling over his recent triumph, which clearly meant a great deal to him.

'I love it,' he said, apropos *Celebrity Big Brother*. 'I got the biggest boos going into the Big Brother house, but the biggest cheers on the way out.'

His life was changing in other ways, too – for a start, he was going to be a lot better off. Alex was not actually being paid for some of the work he was taking part in, namely the Katie reality TV show, but the fact that he was rapidly become very well-known meant that endorsement deals were just round the corner. As for the lack of a pre-nup, that was a good deal more of a risk for Katie, who had a £30 million fortune, than Alex, but even she was decidedly chastened. Aware that her rivalry with Pete had been a big force in the breakdown of the marriage, she was determined it would not happen again: 'I want to buy a house with Alex,' she said. 'I want it all to be equal – his money, my money, completely split down the line. Whatever work we do together, it's not going to be, I take my half, he takes his. We're putting it all in a joint account and that's how a marriage really should be.'

There spoke a woman who had learned from bitter experience. One of the last explosive rows that Katie and Pete had had for their then joint reality show involved exactly that subject – namely money – with Katie insisting that as she earned more than Pete, she should have a greater say in how it was all spent. It was an ugly scene, demeaning to both of them, and certainly not showing her soon-to-be ex-husband much respect. Katie did not want this marriage to go the same way as the last one: yes, it might have been sudden, but she had missed the security that being wed to Pete had given her, and she wasn't going to go down that particular path again.

And Alex was besotted with Katie, no doubt about that. The two might not have spent a great deal of time together since tying the knot, but their body language said it all and he was clearly as excited as a teenager out on a first date when she was around.

In mid-February, they were finally reunited: they were seen dining at the upmarket Japanese restaurant Nobu in London before making their way to a nearby hotel. Both appeared heavily tanned and very glad to be reunited once more.

Of course, Alex had inadvertently added to the furore surrounding the wedding when he admitted that his parents had been a little taken aback. Now he wanted to set the record straight. 'That story was complete nonsense!' he declared. 'My mum and family are 100 per cent behind us and delighted we got married. They all know how incredible Katie is, and we will celebrate with all our family and friends in the UK soon. Being married to Mrs Reid is the most amazing thing in the world: the only bad bit has been having to remove my wedding ring when I'm fighting! I don't like that at all.'

For both of them, this was a new start. Alex was beginning to learn how to cope with life in the limelight while Katie was hoping that the security she craved so badly would now be hers once more. And the children appeared to like and accept Alex, and if they were happy, then everyone was happy.

Well, Pete wasn't always that happy, but he'd accepted what happened and was now trying to move on himself – for there were some further, and quite spectacular, revelations to come.

CHAPTER 14

KATIE AND ALEX
AND PETE

As things began to calm down, everyone managed to start absorbing the new state of affairs: namely, that Katie and Alex were man and wife. What had initially seemed an off-the-cuff decision was now unfolding into hard reality, and it was up to the key players in the drama to accept this and move on.

Although it had been Pete who walked out and initiated the divorce, Katie's sudden marriage must still have been quite a shock. She was, after all, the woman he had married only a few years earlier in the expectation that they would spend the rest of their lives together and he wouldn't have been human, had he not felt the slightest pang at an event that so clearly signalled the end of that earlier dream. No matter what anyone might think about an estranged spouse, breaking up is always sad – and seeing them hook up with another partner even more so.

Indeed, there were some who thought that Pete's tears during the interview with Kate Burley might well have been as a result of his shock at the news that his ex-wife had married again. He himself was insistent that this was not the case and quite the opposite, in fact. 'I wasn't upset because of the wedding, absolutely not,' he declared. 'To me, it was the best closure I could have asked for. Once she became Mrs Reid, it's not my business anymore; I stepped away from the circus a long time ago. Whatever is to do with the kids will be my business.'

His distress had actually been caused by something totally different – namely unexpected criticism from Dwight Yorke, Harvey's biological father: 'Watching a video of Dwight Yorke having a go at me on TV, which I was totally not prepared for, triggered off an emotion,' he explained. 'People were coming up to me today saying, "Just think the best thing to come out of this marriage is two lovely children." I said, "No, three lovely children." That is the way it is. I love Harvey very much and always will.'

As for that much-mooted meeting between himself and Alex, at that point there was no chance. Pete was preparing for a sell-out national tour to start at the end of February, and the last thing he wanted was the distraction of being sucked back into the whole circus surrounding the show. 'I have no problem with him,' he said. 'I've never met the guy. I just don't see a reason why I have to sit down and have a chat at this point.' Instead, his fans were providing him with much-needed support: 'They're not fickle,' declared Pete. 'If you're genuine, they stick with you. I've got the best fans in the world!'

However, he was beginning to move on – quite rapidly, in some ways, as the world was about to discover. Indeed, one thing on his mind had been his tattoo: Katie had a tattoo of Pete's name on her wrist and in the middle of a raucous trip to Ibiza in the wake of the split, she had had it crossed out. Now Pete was beginning to think that it was time for him to rid himself of his own indelible reminder of the relationship. After all, Katie was another man's wife now. 'I think it's time to get rid of the tattoo,' he said. 'I didn't do it before because of the kids. I didn't want them to ask, "Why have you done that?" But now it's the right thing to do.'

Nor did he have any intention of following his ex's example and heading up the aisle again anytime soon: 'It's safe to say it's going to be a long time before I get married,' he said. 'I'm going to keep any relationship private and well away from my children unless it's serious.'

And he was as good as his word: alas, matters were

almost immediately taken out of his control, though. His much-vaunted celibacy wasn't quite the case because to everyone's surprise, at the very end of February, it turned out that he had been having a casual fling. The lucky girl was another former glamour model called Maddy Ford and their relationship, such as it was, had started just over a week after the divorce was finalised. Pete had had enough of living in the middle of a constant circus, which might have been one reason why he had continually insisted in public that there was no one else on the scene. Nor was it remotely serious, which would have been another reason for keeping things under wraps. Whatever the reason, Maddy herself was prepared to go public about it and that's exactly what she did.

Maddy had been a model: now she was a stylist who had worked for Pixie Lott, Brigitte Nielsen and Danielle Lloyd. Pete was not her first famous lover – she once had a fling with Orlando Bloom. But he certainly proved a satisfactory one: 'Pete blew me away in bed,' said thirty-year-old Maddy. 'Every second I was with him, I thought I had died and gone to heaven. His body was incredible and he was so affectionate. I know Jordan once claimed his manhood was the size of an acorn but that is categorically not true. Peter was perfect in every way. But he always liked to be the submissive one. I always wanted him to take charge, but he preferred it when I did. He liked me to be rough with him.'

When this was put to Pete, he had no choice but to admit it. He sounded a little sheepish, too. 'Yes, it's true,' he confessed. 'I was intimate with Maddy on a handful of occasions. We both went into it with our eyes open, and let's just say I certainly know how to pick 'em!'

Pete first met Maddy at a birthday party for one of the children of champion windsurfer Nick Baker and his wife Michelle Clack, who was Maddy's friend. 'Michelle told me Peter was looking for someone who was "the complete opposite" of his ex-wife Katie – and yet he seemed more than interested in me, with my fake boobs and false eyelashes!' Maddy revealed. 'He had already seen my picture on Facebook, thought I was "gorgeous" and wanted to meet me. I thought he would be a useful work contact.'

He soon turned out to be a lot more than that: 'I was quickly introduced to him,' Maddy continued. 'But about an hour later I was at the bar when I sensed someone behind me. It was Peter. He whispered into my neck, "I think you are gorgeous." It was a clumsy chat-up line, but it still sent shudders down my spine. He pulled me over to talk to him in a quiet corner. He quizzed me about my love life, my current status and previous partners – it felt like an interview. Then he left with his children, Junior and Princess. Michelle called me later to say Peter definitely wanted to see me again.'

The result of this was dinner a week later, soon after

which the fling proper began: 'I thought Peter was gorgeous and he clearly thought the same about me,' said Maddy. 'We shared our first kiss in the hallway when Pete had to go at midnight and we swapped numbers. Then we started exchanging sexy texts and pictures – there was no holding back.'

When the relationship was consummated shortly afterwards, a third party was making her presence felt, even though she had no idea at the time what was going on. The ghost of an ex haunts many a new relationship and this one was no exception: Katie and Pete had been one of the world's most public couples and if Katie wasn't there in person, she was certainly around in spirit: 'I felt really nervous about sleeping with him because Katie Price comes across as such a sexual person,' revealed Maddy. 'I thought she was probably an animal in bed. But Pete told me, "It's all an act. She's not like that at all." He told me I had the best body he had ever seen and that my breasts and bum were perfect; he made me feel good. I didn't want to have any secrets or surprises. So I told him I'd once had a fling with Orlando Bloom. I had no idea how Peter was going to react, but he just laughed and told me: "Don't worry, honey. That doesn't worry me at all."'

Indeed, he probably felt relieved: this was someone who had already had a taste of the world of celebrity and knew how to play by the rules – or at least, he thought she did. Given that Pete was still publicly saying there was no one in his life and hadn't been since Katie, he was clearly counting on Maddy to keep her mouth shut. His friends Nick and Michelle knew what was going on, not least because not only had they introduced the couple, but they also had the two round to dinner the following week. The new relationship was consummated in their spare room. They were keeping schtum for the sake of their friend, and Maddy was doing the same while the affair still went on, but her silence wasn't to last.

Indeed, far from it. Once it was out in the open, Maddy seemed keen to share every detail: 'He would never stay the entire night and always left around midnight, after we'd had sex,' she said. 'Most of the time, he was very tender and loving – but he did also like some rough and tumble and roleplay. When we were in bed, he always kept his D&G diamante dog tags on and I'd love grabbing them and rubbing them all over his body. Eventually he gave them to me and said, "Think of me whenever you wear them."

'I wore them every day for a whole month because they smelled of him and his aftershave. He loved it when I sent him a photo of me topless and wearing his dog tags. But in the end, I gave them back to him because I knew he loved them so much.'

And there was much more along the same lines: 'One of his favourite things was to smear me all over with

Coco De Mer edible chocolate body oil and then lick it slowly off – and then to have me do the same to him back again,' said Maddy. 'That was a treat we never tired of. Every time we made love, he liked to put on Sade's *The Love Album* in the background. He especially loved to have sex to the track "This Is No Ordinary Love". He told me to go out and buy the album, and think of him every time I played it. Pete was incredibly romantic like that. He'd do things like light all the candles round his bath before we'd make love but while we'd share the bath, we always retired to his bed for sex. He was obsessed with cleanliness. Every time we were about to have sex, he'd run off to have a shower.'

Maddy only ever went to Pete's Brighton home once: in December 2009. It must have felt as if the relationship was becoming more serious, but in actual fact, it was heading towards the end. 'I sent him lots of naked snaps to keep him keen,' Maddy continued, sounding a little sad. 'I remember how excited he was about giving me a tour round. Then we went up to his bedroom, which is a loft conversion, where we enjoyed a really steamy sex session.'

Maddy met the children, as well as spending time together as a couple with Nick and Michelle but for Pete, the recent past was just too raw. He clearly couldn't face the idea of another really serious relationship just yet. First, he asked her to go away with him and then he changed his mind: 'There were other times when he would sway the other way and tell me he didn't think he was really ready for another relationship,' revealed Maddy. 'Still, he was always ready to have sex with me when it suited him.'

And the relationship was to run a little further: Pete was about to embark on his trip to Australia, but the couple met at Nick and Michelle's before his departure and exchanged seasonal gifts. 'Before he left we met at Michelle and Nick's,' said Maddy. 'I wore special festive red lingerie. Pete always loved my underwear. We had sex and then exchanged presents. I gave him Creed aftershave, which he has worn every day since. I also gave him crystal-encrusted hair straighteners and his favourite Hotel Chocolat chocolate. He gave me a pink video iPod, a bottle of Chanel Coco Mademoiselle, pink cashmere socks from The White Company, MAC make-up and Jo Malone candles, but even when he was away in Australia, he texted me like mad. I sent him lots of naked pictures of myself, which kept him as keen as ever.'

On his return, Pete and Maddy were still working together as well. They got together on a commercial for *Unconditional: Love Songs*, his new album, and a Kia car promotion for a glossy magazine. Matters became steamier still.

'I was dressed in a cropped Alexander McQueen top

that showed my midriff and a cropped leather jacket,' Maddy recalled. 'When Pete arrived, he couldn't take his eyes off me and told me, "You look the sexiest I have ever seen you look!" He kept looking at me, biting his lip and grabbing my bottom. It was unusual for him because we never normally publicly showed that we were gagging for each other. Then all of a sudden he announced that he was going to have a shower. He'd only been gone a few minutes when his brother Mike handed me a towel and told me to take it to Peter. I knocked on the door and as the door opened, Pete pulled me inside. He was totally naked and dripping wet. I was trying to act professional. I had never shagged someone on the job before, but we ended up having sexy, steamy passionate sex right there, up against the wall, in the shower room. It was all over very quickly.'

But that, alas, was that. Pete was still enmeshed in very public rows with his ex-wife, to say nothing of his worries about what would happen as far as the children were concerned, and it was all too much: he simply had too much to lose to get involved at that point. And so Pete called the relationship off, at which point Maddy went public. Pete appeared pretty embarrassed about it all, too.

'I always said that I would only talk about a new relationship if it was a serious one, and as far as I'm concerned this was not serious,' he said. 'I have tried in my heart to do everything in the right way. I waited until

I was divorced before I considered moving on. I have never been intimate with anyone in front of my children, apart from their mother to this day. I remained faithful to my ex-wife throughout our marriage until I was divorced. As far as I am concerned, I am a single guy without a girlfriend.'

Which was fair enough. The only problem was that Pete had made quite a song and dance about being celibate, something he continued to talk about after the fling with Maddy had begun. No one was in the slightest bit of doubt that Pete was, and remains an extremely decent man, but he had created a hostage to fortune for himself and now he was paying the price.

Newspapers were not slow to put it to him that he had been saying one thing and doing quite another. So, Pete held up his hands: 'I dipped my toe in the water and got burnt,' he admitted. 'Yes, I had sex, but only after my divorce came through and I always said that I would not think about moving on until after my divorce was finalised. I dipped my toe back into the water and got badly burnt. What a mistake that was! I'm gutted. But I've got it out of my system. I don't want to go there with anyone else again now, not unless I know it's serious. The children are my priority, and always will be – not a new woman.'

Indeed, most people remained deeply sympathetic. Pete was still perceived to have been something of the victim in the break-up of the relationship, and given that he was now a free man, he could do whatever he liked. Also, to put it bluntly, he'd been celibate for quite some time before getting together with Maddy – hardly surprising that he felt the need for some form of release. And he had certainly never wavered in his desire to do all he could to protect his children: nothing had changed there at all.

Katie, however, was absolutely livid to discover there had been someone else in the background for the last few months. She was fed up with being painted as the villain in the relationship, claims backed up by the fact that she had moved on so fast and met someone else so soon, and she was sick of hearing about the goodness of Saint Pete. This, to her, was vindication that it wasn't such a one-sided story after all and that Pete might have been as much at fault as Katie. Indeed, the story also emerged very shortly after Pete had spoken about his feelings over her relationship (or lack of it) with Andrew Gould, and it made her see red.

'He's been saying he hasn't had sex, but all along he has,' she told a friend. 'He's made out like he's got this whiter-than-white image, but he's no saint!' In a strange way, however, just as her marriage gave Pete some kind of closure, the revelations might be said to do the same for Katie. Both of them had been involved with other people – even if, in Pete's case, it didn't amount to anything much: now, they could move on.

And Katie certainly wanted to do so. She caused her advisors a certain degree of alarm when it emerged that she wanted to be known as Katie Reid: in terms of business, this did not make sense. Katie already operated under two monikers, Jordan and Katie Price, and she'd become famous using the two of them as a type of brand. To change her name now would just confuse everyone and have a deleterious effect upon sales.

'She is absolutely besotted with Alex and wants to be known as Katie Reid to everyone,' said a source. 'But she has been told it is simply not a good business idea. She is pretty upset about it because she wants to prove to the world that she really does love Alex. A meeting was held to discuss forthcoming projects when she brought her request up. She was pretty peed off when she was told that it wouldn't be a sensible thing to do.'

But given that her company was called Pricey Media, her novels and pony books came out under the name Katie Price and her riding range was known as KP Equestrian, this really made no sense. 'Jordan is a shrewd businesswoman,' observed the source. 'She has cleverly taken advantage of every opportunity that has come her way and has made a fortune. All she is now being told by her advisers is to protect that.'

Indeed, and Katie was no fool when it came to money for who knew what the future held?

CHAPTER 15

KATIE AND ALEX

Way back when they first got together, Katie and Pete were the perfect couple for the age we live in today. Both attractive, media-savvy and prepared to live out their lives in the glare of the television camera, they were the people's version of Prince Charles and Princess Diana – and in the end, their relationship proved just as doomed as that of the Prince and the Princess, over a decade before.

So, what was the reason for the break-up? Ultimately, a million reasons, and none at all: whatever the rows about Andrew Gould, and who earned more, who was the most famous and who got to dictate everything they did, they were unsuited. Katie is two people: Katie Price and Jordan, and while the Katie side might be closer to the reality, Jordan still exists – and Pete couldn't cope with that. A family man, with a taste for domesticity, he didn't want to go out and party every night. Neither did Katie, but Jordan did.

When she met Alex, Katie was in a very different frame of mind. Fresh from the shock of the break-up with Pete, she was still very vulnerable and indeed, on paper, a cross-dressing cage fighter would not necessarily come across as ideal husband material. But in actual fact, Alex has proved to be far more than that: his stint on *Celebrity Big Brother* did exactly what Katie wanted it to, showing him to be a fundamentally decent man who had been dragged into the whirlwind of publicity surrounding her and forced to learn quickly how to cope.

But there was one crucial difference in this meeting, as well: Alex got to know both Katie and Jordan right from the start and seems capable of dealing with both. Nor do the two seem so very dissimilar. Both are fundamentally family people, yet both enjoy the glitz and glamour of the showbiz lifestyle as much as anyone. They both like quiet nights in, but they also enjoy wild nights out. At the moment, at least, they seem in tune with each other, although there's no way of knowing if that will last.

Another crucial element in it all is that Alex doesn't appear to mind Katie calling all the shots. Katie is clearly a woman who needs to be in control of every aspect of her life, and that includes her relationships. In the end, it became all too much for Pete. But Alex, who has seen his profile rocket since meeting Katie (and that is another difference from Pete, who was already a name in his own right), does not appear to object to her deciding what the two of them will be doing – and why should he? She's created an astonishingly successful career for herself.

Clearly, the next project on the cards is children: both have expressed a desire to have a family, and as Katie is only thirty-one, there should be no difficulties there. Nor should there be any problems in the upbringing of her children from Dwight and Pete: Alex has shown that he is more than willing to look after them and get on with them, but he clearly wants a brood of his own.

As for their career, it looks set to grow bigger than ever. Katie has become an icon of our times, a figure of complete fascination who can sell out a magazine run just by appearing on the cover, and there looks to be no end in sight to all of that. It's something she has in common with Princess Diana: that men lust after her and women relate to her. Somehow both exude an empathetic quality, for Katie's life has by no means been a straightforward one. Apart from her tempestuous love life, she's had plenty of nonsense to deal with throughout her lifetime and other women can sympathise with that.

And whatever anyone thinks of her – and she does

divide opinion pretty sharply – Katie has made something of her life. She's come from a fairly humble background to become one of the best known and most talked-about women in the country. The story of Katie – and Alex – will run and run.